IMAGES
of America

LATINOS IN MILWAUKEE

Established as Holy Trinity School in 1850 for the German-speaking community, Bruce-Guadalupe Community School has long served bilingual students. As demographics shifted, so did the school's focus. Today Bruce-Guadalupe primarily serves the Spanish-speaking community. The school merged with the United Community Center (UCC) in 1990. Among the students shown in this 1956 photograph is young Joe Monreal (second row, far left). ¿Y qué?

On the cover: Latino immigrants in the 1930s and 1940s worked hard to maintain their cultural identity. The Cuadro Dramático Anahuac, of Sociedad Mutualista Hispano-Azteca, produced plays and musicals from Mexico. Shown in this 1940 photograph are, from left to right, (front row) Concepción Sierra, Jesucita Sierra, Rita Mariscal, and Eladio Palomino; (second row) José Schlemm, Donato Paniagua, Federico Herrera, Rafael Pérez, Rodolfo Schlemm, David Valdes, Trinidad López, and Antonio Chávez. (Photograph from the collection of Arnoldo Sevilla.)

IMAGES
of America

LATINOS IN MILWAUKEE

Joseph A. Rodriguez, Ph.D., and Walter Sava, Ph.D.

ARCADIA
PUBLISHING

Published by Arcadia Publishing
Charleston, South Carolina

Library of Congress Catalog Card Number: 2006923715

For all general information contact Arcadia Publishing at:
Telephone 843-853-2070
Fax 843-853-0044
E-mail sales@arcadiapublishing.com
For customer service and orders:
Toll-Free 1-888-313-2665

Visit us on the Internet at www.arcadiapublishing.com

To my loving family, Beth, Cristina, Antonio, and Leah.
—Joseph A. Rodriguez, Ph.D.

To my son, Carlos, the joy of my life.
—Walter Sava, Ph.D.

CONTENTS

ACKNOWLEDGMENTS

When Miguel Sevilla Chávez, among Milwaukee's early Latino immigrants, returned to Mexico during the Great Depression, he never dreamed that one of his future children would return to the city and become the Latino community's unofficial historian. Arnoldo Sevilla's amazing collection of photographs, passion for local history, and unflagging enthusiasm have been vital to this book. We could not have done it without him. *¡Mil gracias, Arnoldo!*

We also thank Gregory Smith, who embraced the project, wrote many of the captions, and coordinated the work of student researchers Martin Christiansen, Theresa Coronado, Nicholas Papakis, and Drew Zoellick. With his Guatemala-born wife, Esperanza, and their family, the Smiths are part of the "next chapter" in the history of Latinos in Milwaukee.

Many thanks to the United Community Center, Ricardo Díaz, José Olivieri, and José Vásquez. We also thank graphic artist María Fontanez Ruiz, the staff of Latino Arts Incorporated, the *Milwaukee Journal-Sentinel*, and the Roberto Hernández Center at the University of Wisconsin–Milwaukee.

Muchísimas gracias to the Board of Directors of the Latino Historical Society of Wisconsin: Juan Alvarez Cuahtémoc, Tony Báez, M. Lourdes Castillo, René Farías, Rafael Fernández, Raúl Galván, Eloísa Gómez, Rose Guajardo, Geary Morales, Roberto Nodal, Jertha Ramos-Colón, Cipriano Sánchez, Arnoldo Sevilla, John Torres, and Olga Valcourt-Schwartz.

The project was funded in part by a grant from the Wisconsin Humanities Council, with funds from the National Endowment for the Humanities and the State of Wisconsin. Any views, findings, conclusions, or recommendations expressed in this project do not necessarily represent those of the National Endowment for the Humanities.

Special thanks are extended to all who shared treasured family photographs and stories—our communal story. Finally, we are forever grateful to *los antepasados*, our Latino ancestors, who left their homes and family members to come to Milwaukee. They have shaped our community's history with their courage, vision, and hard work.

INTRODUCTION

Latinos have resided in Milwaukee since at least the 1880s when Mexican immigrant Rafael Báez settled here and became a music teacher at Marquette University. Most Latinos, however, came to the area as common laborers, performing hard and dirty work in factories, foundries, railroads, and fields. Although Milwaukee-area Latinos have been primarily concentrated in the city's south side and the Riverwest neighborhoods, many have dispersed throughout Milwaukee and are increasingly moving to the suburban communities of South Milwaukee, Cudahy, St. Francis, and Oak Creek. Still, the south side is visually identified as the Latino community, and, aptly, South Sixteenth Street was renamed César E. Chávez Drive in honor of the labor leader who inspired activists beginning in the 1960s.

This book of historic photographs documents the history of a growing community. While Milwaukee's overall population declined by five percent between 1990 and 2000, the city's Latino population grew by 82 percent and today is estimated at more than 100,000. This rapid growth came from natural birth, immigration from Latin America, and migration from other parts of the United States. For many, coming to Milwaukee represented a change for the better. Latinos have revived the south side neighborhoods where once eastern Europeans, primarily Polish Americans, resided. Latino commercial energy is seen in the bustling shopping areas of César E. Chávez Drive, National Avenue, and Mitchell Street.

Many Latino families shared photographs and stories of their families and friends, most of which are published for the first time. These stories tell of persistence against great odds. They tell of young families leaving their homelands, trekking across borders by foot, by boat, by train, or by airplane, and coming to Milwaukee in search of a better life. The stories tell of how Latinos have struggled to find work and to support their families. The heroes of the stories are not only the acknowledged community leaders but the parents and teachers who, in difficult circumstances, raised children to respect two cultures and become contributing members of society—the founders of businesses, social organizations, artists, doctors, writers, and activists.

Over a three-month period in 1980, Milwaukee native Robert Glick created a series of 43 black-and-white photographs entitled Hispanic Vistas. The project, with the backing of the City of Milwaukee CETA Arts Program, featured outstanding portrayals of the Latino community in Milwaukee, including this touching depiction of two young girls sharing secrets and giggling on the sofa in their mother's living room.

These buildings on South Fifth Street in Milwaukee are remembered as having housed a series of Latino grocery stores, including the first in the Milwaukee area, Morales', which opened in 1926. This Robert Glick photograph depicts the store (Casa Martínez/Rubén's Quality Foods) while undergoing renovations that would connect the two buildings, expanding its size. The buildings have since been razed.

One

LOS PRIMEROS

The early Latino settlers in the Milwaukee community were the pioneers, or *los primeros*. The earliest primero, Rafael Báez, arrived in 1884 and became a music teacher at Marquette University. In 1922, the Pfister-Vogel tannery on South Sixth Street recruited about 100 Mexican men to take the jobs of striking Anglos. The Mexicans came as contract workers from the town of Tangancicuaro, Michoacán. Undoubtedly, tensions were created when Mexicans crossed the picket line, but the Mexicans needed the work. They initially slept in a dormitory set up in the tannery before finding housing in the nearby community.

Other primeros worked for the railroad. Most primeros settled in the Walker's Point area, convenient to jobs in the foundries and tanneries. The housing was less than ideal, but the rent was acceptable, and the numerous Catholic churches provided some cultural continuity. Many were *solteros*, or young, single men, who left Mexico but planned to return. Some would settle permanently and marry local women of Polish and German ancestry. Mexican primeros dealt with discrimination and poverty by turning inward and formed societies known as *mutualistas*. Club Mexicano provided fellowship, social support, and connections to the homeland.

The Puerto Rican primeros arrived in the late 1940s, with most coming to Milwaukee directly from the island. Some had previously worked as migrant farmworkers in Michigan before settling in Milwaukee, where they found factory work. Like the Mexican primeros, Puerto Ricans formed hometown clubs celebrating the people and culture of the towns of their birthplace on the island. Between 1960 and 1970, Milwaukee's Puerto Rican population grew from 2,820 to 5,889. Initially they settled in the poor area of the Third Ward and in Yankee Hill on the east side, but freeway construction forced them to relocate to Riverwest area in the 1970s.

Cubans arrived first in the early 1960s and later in the early 1980s, following the exodus of the Marielito refugees, who first came to Fort McCoy and then dispersed throughout the state. More recently, groups of South and Central Americans have settled in the city, fleeing political turmoil in their homelands.

In 1884, Mexican musician and composer Rafael Báez arrived in Milwaukee and married into a noted German family. He developed a successful career as one of the city's finest organists, playing at Gesu Church, St. John's, Temple Emanu-El, and a local opera company. Báez was the first Latino teacher at Marquette University, where he taught music.

By 1927, Carlos Durán had been in Milwaukee for five years and had earned enough money to purchase the family's first car, a 1923 Cadillac. The Durán children, three of whom were born in Milwaukee, pose for a photograph while on an outing to Juneau Park at the lakefront. Shown here are, from left to right, (front) Margarita, Petrita (with dog), Ruth, and Amelia; (rear) María (with doll) and Anita (standing on the running board).

Like many early Mexican immigrants, Jesús Padilla Escobar left his family until he could send for them later. Delfina Rodríguez de Padilla rejoined her husband in August 1923, making the trip north with Ramona Durán, Juanita Niño, and the Padillas' three children: Ramona, Delfina, and Esther. Tragically, Jesús Padilla drowned in Lake Michigan in 1929 while on a family picnic.

Federico Herrera, a 22-year-old Mexican immigrant, settled in Milwaukee in 1925 after playing baseball in Texas for the owners of Mexico's Dos Estrellas mines. With Miguel Sevilla Chávez and Jesús C. Pérez, in 1930, he cofounded Círculo Social de Amigos "Emilio Carranza," honoring the first Mexican to pilot a plane between Mexico City and Washington, D.C. He also founded Milwaukee's first Spanish-language newspapers, *Sancho Panza* and *Boletín Informativo*.

Jesús Martínez fled the Mexican Revolution in 1914, leaving Michoacán, Mexico, and settled in Milwaukee in 1923. He was involved in the Círculo Social de Amigos "Emilio Carranza" and ran a boardinghouse for Mexican immigrants. Pictured in this 1926 photograph from left to right are David Valdes Jr., Gregorio Schlemm, a girl identified only as "daughter of Mr. Arciniéga," Martínez's sister Mrs. Martínez de Schlemm (with baby son Malaquías), Mariano Schlemm (on tricycle), Jesús Martínez (with daughter María Luisa), his wife Adela "Chona" Anaya de Martínez, and daughters María Jesusita and Maximiliana Martínez.

With travel both expensive and difficult, Latino immigrants made family portraits a priority because they were able to showcase new family members and the family's success to friends and relatives in their native countries. In this classic 1926 family photograph, Luciano and Norberta Haro, immigrants from Tepechitlán, Zacatecas, Mexico, pose with sons Jesse and Marcos and daughter Antonia.

Oppression of the Catholic Church in Mexico provoked armed insurrection by a group that became known as Los Cristeros. Like thousands of others, in 1926, Miguel Sevilla Chávez fled his country. He settled in Milwaukee, where he cofounded Círculo Social de Amigos "Emilio Carranza," along with Milwaukee's first Spanish-language newspapers, *Sancho Panza* and *Boletín Informativo*.

Many Mexican immigrants in Milwaukee in the 1920s were *solteros*, unmarried young men. Some, including Miguel Sevilla Chávez, found wives of other nationalities. He married Ana Wrobel, a girl of Polish heritage, in 1930. The Sevillas moved to Michoacán, Mexico, in 1932, where they had 12 children, all born in Mexico. Four of the Sevilla children in this 1949 photograph later settled in Milwaukee.

In 1924, Knights of Columbus members helped form Club Mexicano, Milwaukee's first Latino social organization. Pictured from left to right are (first row) Juan Santos Herrera (treasurer), Ricardo Mijares (secretary), Ismael Cárdenas (president), Manuel Flores (vice president), and Manuel Martínez (pro secretary); (second row) Fausto Regalado, Frank Gross (the Knights of Columbus "Mexican Ambassador" to the *colonia*), Mariano Niño, Robert Witting, William G. Bruce (also of the Knights of Columbus), and Jesús Lara.

David and Catalina Valdes settled in Milwaukee in the 1920s and in 1928 posed for this family photograph, later presented as a gift to David's *compadre* (godfather) Jesús Martínez. From left to right are David Valdes, David Jr. (standing), and Catalina Valdes, with daughter Catalina on her lap.

With a significant number of Latino immigrants already in Milwaukee in the 1920s, Alberto Castro, Celedonio Rodríguez, and others formed Sociedad Mutualista Hispano-Azteca, a mutual aid association that promoted a sense of community by celebrating Mexican holidays and community advocacy. This is an illustration of the organization's fifth anniversary in 1935.

Eleuterio and Raquel Valdovinos emigrated from Mexico to Milwaukee in 1930. This 1937 photograph depicts their children, from left to right, Raquel, Eleuterio, Ramiro, Reynaldo, Rodrigo, Gustavo, and Salvador. Not pictured is older sister Beatriz. The four youngest children were born in Milwaukee, while the four oldest were born in Mexico.

In 1924, Francisco González, born in Zacatecas, Mexico, joined Club Mexicano, the city's first Mexican social organization. By decade's end, he had met 15-year-old Eleuteria Ruano, also originally from Zacatecas, and the couple married in 1930. This 1939 photograph shows the González family in their South Third Street home. From left to right are Francisco, Luciano, Florencio, Francisco "Frank" Jr., Josephine, Eleuteria, and María.

Virtually every immigrant group has valued education, and the family of Ramón Talamantes was no exception. Three of the Talamantes girls, Celia, Emerita, and Lydia, pose for this portrait to commemorate their joint 1940 graduation from Mercy High School, located at Twenty-Ninth and Mitchell Streets.

Believing that it was missing out on federal money for services due to undercounting of Hispanics in the 1980 U.S. Census, the City of Milwaukee held a special census from April 3 to 15, 1985. Advance publicity featured a brochure and a Robert Glick photograph of the four-generation family of Fidel and Eloisa Gómez, who emigrated from central Mexico in the 1920s and settled on Milwaukee's south side in the late 1940s.

Peter Sandoval Sr., born in Mexico in 1906, moved to Milwaukee as a teenager. An accomplished musician, Sandoval played for the José Martínez and Allis-Chalmers Orchestras and the John Anello Choir. He worked at Allis-Chalmers for 34 years, raised seven children, and helped found Our Lady of Guadalupe Church. Sandoval is pictured here at home, holding two of his children after the Great Snowstorm of 1947.

Fluent in German, Spanish-born Antonio Roca settled in Milwaukee to sell fruits and nuts to German immigrants. Over the years, he sold his goods from seven different store locations. In this March 1952 photograph, he is standing inside his last store at 735 West Wisconsin Avenue. The store was closed when the building was sold to build Continental Savings Bank. Roca eventually moved to Tegucigalpa, Honduras, to establish a Baha'i temple.

Emelia Vásquez de Rivera left a remote mountain village near Comerío, Puerto Rico, to settle in Milwaukee in 1953 with her four children: José, Perfecto, Lydia, and Julio. A single mother, Emelia remarried in 1959, becoming the wife of Juan Ferreira, with whom she had three additional children: Emily, Jenny, and Nilda.

In the late 1940s, Milwaukee's first major Puerto Rican neighborhood was on the northeast side of the city. By 1960, it had become home to the city's greatest concentration of Puerto Ricans. Urban renewal later forced the group to move to the neighborhood now known as Riverwest. There the group maintained many deep-rooted Puerto Rican customs, such as house parties, *quinceañeras*, the gift of *capias* (ribbon souvenirs from parties), and *parranda* (a special form of Christmas caroling). This 1980 Robert Glick photograph depicts Amelia Figueroa and Angel Díaz, immigrants from Puerto Rico in the mid-1950s. Having already retired, they settled in a Puerto Rican neighborhood on the north side of town, and Angel supplemented his pension by selling fruits and vegetables door-to-door. The couple had four children, 24 grandchildren, and at least 72 great-grandchildren.

María "Mary" Báez, daughter of Rafael Báez, was the first woman of Mexican origin to be born and raised in Milwaukee. Her father moved to Milwaukee in 1884, having been recruited by the C. D. Hess Opera Company, a precursor of the Florentine Opera Company. Mary passed away in 1988 at the age of 92. (Courtesy of the Milwaukee Journal-Sentinel.)

Two

WORK

Many of Milwaukee's Latinos first came to Wisconsin as migrant workers. Mexicans came from Texas to Wisconsin to pick apples, cherries, and sugar beets. Laboring in the hot sun, stooping over, and picking crops for little pay was difficult work. However, with little work in the summer in Texas, migrants returned to Texas in the fall. The trips were long and arduous. They came as families and had to support themselves on the road. One of their most important possessions was an automobile or truck that provided basic transportation. Fieldwork was often a family occupation, in which adults and children alike picked crops and earned a "piece rate" that contributed to the family economy. Living conditions were rudimentary, yet despite the poor conditions, Mexican families sometimes forged strong relationships with farm owners and returned annually to work in the same fields.

Early migrants also worked on the railroad. The so-called *traquistas* built boxcars and maintained railroad tracks throughout the United States. In Milwaukee, railroad workers arrived in the 1920s and for a while lived in boxcars.

The most fortunate workers found year-round jobs in manufacturing, where the factory pay was better than working in the fields. Manufacturing jobs allowed Mexicans and, later, Puerto Ricans to drop out of the migrant stream and stop uprooting children from schools. Their children could then attend the same school all year round. Although jobs in tanneries and foundries paid better, the work was more physically demanding. The factories were cold in the winter and hot in the summer. Tannery work was especially dirty, and the caustic acids burned the skin and irritated the eyes and nose. Latinos were relegated to the worst jobs and the lowest pay. With better education, there is an already sizable and growing Latino professional class. Today many Latinos have moved out of poverty and into the middle class.

In the 1940s, Espiridión "Poloy" Martínez and María de Jesús "Chita" Flores worked as migrant workers, traveling between Eagle Pass, Texas, and Wind Lake, Wisconsin, every year for the harvests. Their daughter Irene Santos stayed in Milwaukee permanently, working with United Migrant Opportunity Services (UMOS), Centro Hispano, and eventually began a social services counseling business for Spanish speakers in Racine. This 1923 photograph depicts her parents on their wedding day.

Before settling in Milwaukee, the Alvarez family of San Antonio, Texas, worked picking apples, cherries, and sugar beets. Every year they would journey from Texas to Michigan, Illinois, then Iowa, and on to Wisconsin before returning home. This 1935 photograph shows members of the family while working in Door County, Wisconsin. From left to right are Ventura Alvarez, Rosa Alvarez, Jerónimo Alvarez, Apolonio "Polo" Alvarez, and Leonor Hernández de Alvarez.

With a labor shortage caused by a strike in 1922, Pfister and Vogel contracted Mexican workers in southern Texas and northern Mexico to work in their tannery and the railroad yet kept them totally uninformed about being hired as replacement workers. Many of the workers lived close to the railroads and tanneries on Milwaukee's south side. This 1940 photograph includes worker Alberto Castro (seated, fourth from left).

With their parents constantly moving from state to state, children of migrant workers often attended several different schools throughout the school year. This 1943 photograph of the students at Apple School at North Cape, Wisconsin, pictures many sons and daughters of Mexican migrant workers, including those of Poloy Martínez and Chita Flores.

By the 1940s, many Latino women were working in the garment industry, which has long depended on the sweat of immigrant workers. Angie Ramos, who worked in a Milwaukee garment factory sewing jackets, is pictured center row, fourth from left, in this 1943 photograph of all-stars from women's baseball teams sponsored by the International Ladies Garment Workers Union, founded in 1900.

In this 1949 photograph, from left to right, migrant workers Elodia Martínez, Genevieve Flores, Margarita Martínez, and Marta Martínez take a Saturday break from fieldwork. The four young women were surely anticipating that evening's open-air dance to be held on a concrete warehouse slab at a farm near Wind Lake.

After the final harvest, most migrant workers departed Wisconsin just before the cold winter months. This photograph depicts the Roiz family, originally from Crystal City, Texas, while working near Wind Lake, Wisconsin, in 1949.

Many Latino immigrants found work in area tanneries, including 32-year-old Sacramento Delgadillo, who came to Milwaukee in 1956 from Zacatecas, Mexico. His wife, Amalia, joined him 18 months later, and the couple raised eight children. Delgadillo worked double shifts for the next 30 years, retiring from Gebhard-Vogel in 1986.

By World War I, Pfister and Vogel was the world's largest tannery. In 1922, the company experienced a violent labor strike and sent labor agents to Mexico to recruit workers, who were intentionally kept unaware that they would be strikebreakers. In this 1959 photograph, from left to right are John Wheels, Gerónimo Rivas, José Pérez, John Nuck, Antonio Andrade, and Samuel Martínez. The company closed its operations in Milwaukee in February 2000, laying off 600 employees.

Francisco José Lamelas Blanco (right, facing camera) joined his father's Havana law practice in 1941 but fled Cuba for the United States in 1961. Lamelas worked menial jobs before bringing his family to Racine in 1964 and then to Milwaukee, where he worked as a bank loan officer and later a juvenile probation officer. In this 1959 baptism photograph, daughter Elsa holds her brother Francisco. The children's mother, Elsa Salazar de Lamelas, stands at left with daughter Blanca Margarita (arms folded).

26

Post–World War II industrial growth and subsequent demand for labor opened an era of opportunity for Latinos such as Pablo Borda, pictured in 1965, who came to the United States from Chile in 1960 and worked as a skilled machinist at Louis Allis. A grand knight of the Knights of Columbus, Borda was a leader of the Cursillo Movement in the Catholic Church and cofounder and past president of the Latino Soccer Club.

The family of Cipriano and María Gregoria Sánchez came to the United States from Tampico, Tamaulipas, Mexico, as migrant workers before settling in Milwaukee. Picking cucumbers in 1967 at the Marks Brothers Pickle Company near Wautoma, Wisconsin, are, from left to right, Raymunda Sánchez (age 19), Juana Sánchez (age 15), and Cipriano "Tano" Sánchez Jr. (age 17). Their father, Cipriano Sánchez Sr., is in the background. Tano became well known in the Milwaukee community as the founder of the Aztec Warriors Soccer Club.

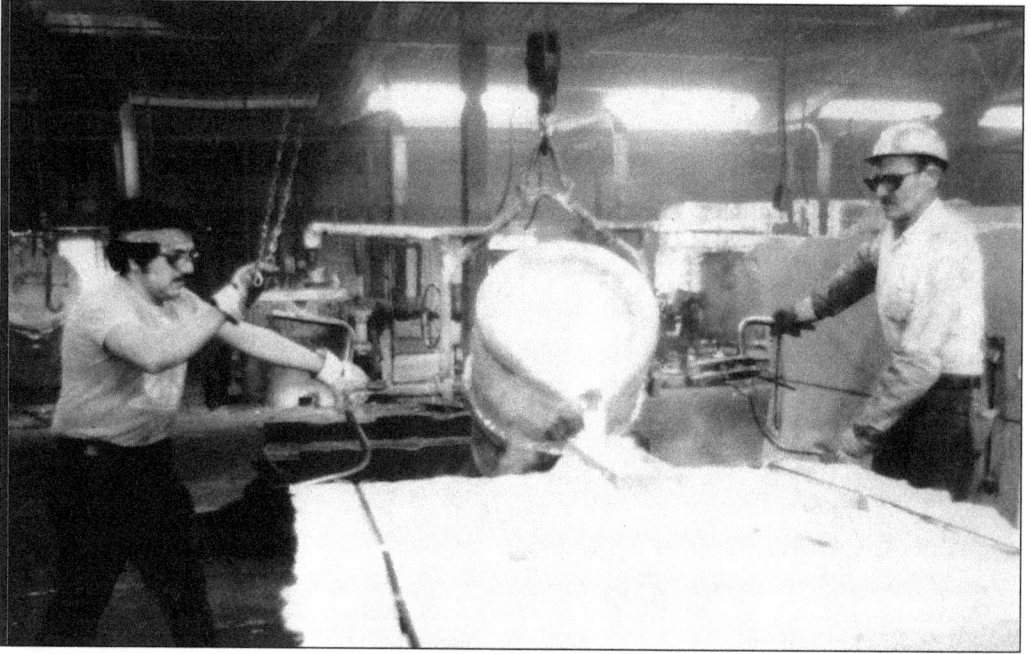

Foundry work is hot, dirty, and dangerous. Nevertheless, Latino immigrants, eager to advance the standards of living for their families, helped form the backbone of Milwaukee foundries. Javier Sánchez, at left in this c. 1970 photograph, supported his family and raised nine children as a foundry worker for many years.

The steadily increasing number of Latino firefighters and police officers has significantly reduced problems relating to language barriers, helping to save many lives over the years. In this 1978 photograph, Milwaukee firefighter Estevan Quesada meets with a child development class from UMOS, explaining what to do in case of fire. (Courtesy of the Milwaukee Journal-Sentinel.)

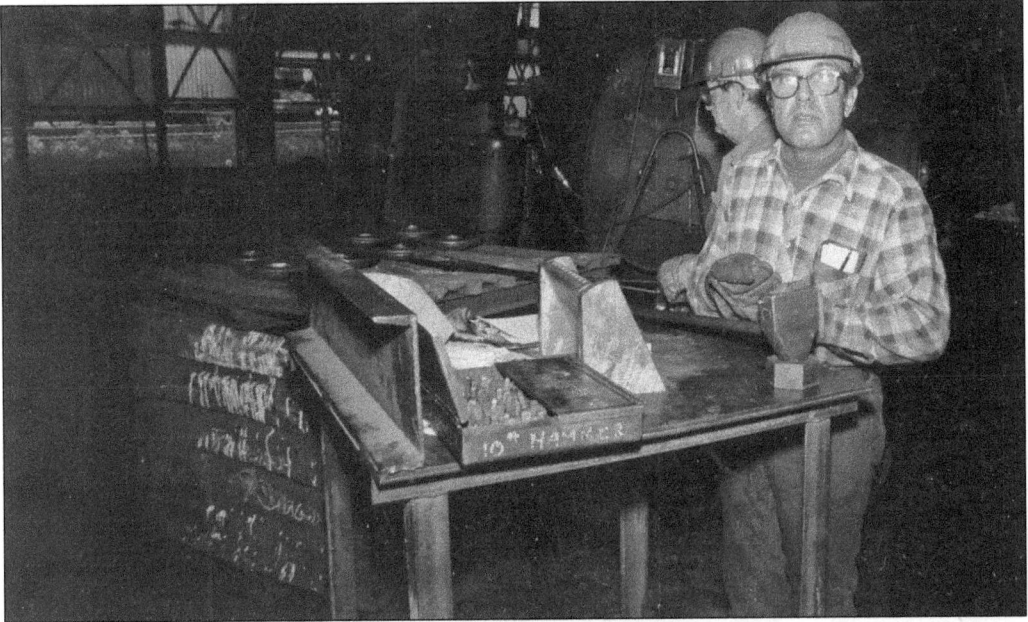

Antonio and Ralph Analla, sons of Raphael and Luz Analla, who came to the United States from Mexico in January 1919, were the first set of brothers to enter the Milwaukee's Golden Gloves tournament in January 1948. Antonio fought at the 126-pound rank, while Ralph was a contender for the 147-pound open division. In this 1980s photograph, Antonio (right) is shown stamping serial numbers on forgings at the Ladish Company.

The Milwaukee area has been blessed by the dedication and hard work of Latino teachers, principals, and administrators. Pictured here, from left to right, are four of the first Latinos to serve as Milwaukee Public Schools principals: Lourdes Castillo, Fermín Burgos, Rose Guajardo, and Isidro Villa.

Born in Venezuela, Dr. Leonardo Aponte studied medicine in Rome, Italy. He later moved to Germany, married, and raised four children. In 1974, the family moved to Milwaukee and Aponte opened his clinic on South Sixteenth Street. Aponte is well known and respected in Milwaukee for his compassion and generosity in providing care to patients who cannot afford treatment.

In 1989, Philip Arreola was the first Latino ever appointed as Milwaukee's police chief and served until 1996, when he was named the police chief of Tacoma, Washington. Arreola maintains close Milwaukee ties, sponsoring a scholarship fund through the Hispanic Chamber of Commerce-Wisconsin. Parade marshal of the 1991 Mexican Independence Day parade, he is pictured marching with the Aztec Warriors Soccer Club and the Latino Sports Association of Wisconsin.

Three

BUSINESS

As Milwaukee's Latino community grew, entrepreneurs realized that newcomers desired a taste of the old country and soon opened restaurants, grocery stores, bars, and bakeries. Initially these Latino-owned businesses were small affairs, serving mostly the Latino migrant and immigrant population of the south side. However, some grew with the community and now serve Latinos and non-Latinos alike, have multiple locations and numerous employees, and earn revenues in the millions.

In Milwaukee, the major Latino-owned businesses include restaurants, grocery stores, music and video stores, apparel stores, and travel agencies. The commercial streets of National Avenue, Mitchell Street, and César E. Chávez Drive show the hustle and bustle of the Latino influence. Stores reflect the cultural realities of the Latino community. Many shops sell baby clothes and *quinceañera* dresses. During late October, south side bakeries sell *pan de muerto*, or "Day of the Dead bread," as part of the Día de los Muertos celebration (All Saints' Day). Grocery stores sell many varieties of chilies used in Latin American cuisine. Supermercado El Rey, the largest Latino-owned grocery store chain in the state, is adorned with piñatas. Connections to the homeland continue, as evidenced by the large number of stores that offer money-wiring services.

Entrepreneurialism is important because many immigrants come without knowing English. Others, particularly doctors and lawyers, are well educated but find it difficult to gain access to their old professions. Opening a business that caters to the immigrant or Spanish-speaking population has always been a viable employment alternative and helps the community by hiring Latino employees.

Historically, Latino-owned businesses also served as information centers and helped solidify the community's cultural retention. Latino newcomers to Milwaukee could learn information about housing and employment by dropping in at a south side tavern or restaurant. Taverns sponsored bowling and softball leagues and billiards and dominoes tournaments. From Conejitos to El Rey, El Farol, and La Fuente, Latino groceries and restaurateurs have added a special flavor to the city that is enjoyed by all Milwaukee residents.

Luciano Haro, a 30-year-old Mexican immigrant to Milwaukee, took a few minutes to pose (left, behind counter) for a photograph with several of his customers in 1931. The grocery store was located in the 500 block of South Fifth Street. Haro's daughter Mary, then three years old, timidly looks into the store from the back room.

José Cárdenas opened one of the city's first Mexican grocery stores in 1940 at the corner of Sixth and Walker Streets and operated the store until 1963, when he retired, selling the store to make way for the Interstate 94 freeway construction. Mercedes "Mariquita" Cárdenas, José's wife, poses for this photograph with their son Emery Cárdenas in 1946.

Pedro Cruz, who moved to Milwaukee from Puerto Rico in the early 1950s, was one of the first Puerto Rican immigrants in Milwaukee to open a tavern, the Juana Díaz Tavern. Shown in this Robert Glick photograph, the tavern sponsored community billiard tournaments, softball and baseball tournaments, and a dominoes league.

In 1962, the Monreal family opened El Matador restaurant at the intersection of South Sixth and Bruce Streets. The restaurant soon became a prominent and long-lasting Latino business in the city. With the management of María de la Luz Monreal, matriarch of this notable Milwaukee Latino family, El Matador's success was the result of its high quality and great service.

In the early 1970s, Pedro and Gloria Castillo opened Pedrano's, a popular Mexican restaurant in the building formerly occupied by the Monreal family's El Matador. Their new business helped cement the neighborhood around South Sixth and Bruce Streets as a well-known dining destination. The Castillos, on the dance floor in this *c.* 1973 photograph, were also involved in early Latino dance groups and soccer clubs.

The son of a baker, José López Sr. (center) immigrated to Houston, Texas, from Mexico in 1967. In 1968, he met Consuelo Arucha de Segovia, who contracted him to work in her bakery in Milwaukee. In 1978, Rubén Martínez allowed López to set up a bakery in the back of the Casa Martínez store and eventually helped him move into his own storefront. López Bakery currently operates five locations.

José "Conejito" González, who arrived in Milwaukee in 1957 from Mexico with $20 in his pocket, describes being turned down for a tannery job as the luckiest day in his life. In 1968, he opened a tavern at 714 South Sixth Street, which later relocated to South Fifth and Virginia Streets, adding a *comedor* (dining room). Conejito's Place is a popular south side fixture, frequented by people from all walks of life.

Milwaukee's first Puerto Rican parade celebrating San Juan Bautista Day traveled along Wisconsin Avenue from Tenth Street to the lakefront. By 1979, the parade had moved to Holton Street. A market at 2029 North Holton Street, originally Rosario's, then Bodega Latina, and now Pueblo Supermarket, has served the surrounding Puerto Rican neighborhood for decades. Liduina Estramera, owner since 1989, expanded the store in 1996 to serve the community even better.

In 1969, Rubén Martínez (left) and John Alvarado founded the Latin American Chamber of Commerce, which incorporated as the Hispanic Chamber of Commerce of Wisconsin in 1972. Martínez owned one of the oldest Mexican grocery stores in Milwaukee, Casa Martínez, while Alvarado was a popular barber and owner of the Cross Keys Barbershop. Martínez and Alvarado are pictured in the 1972 Mexican Independence Day parade.

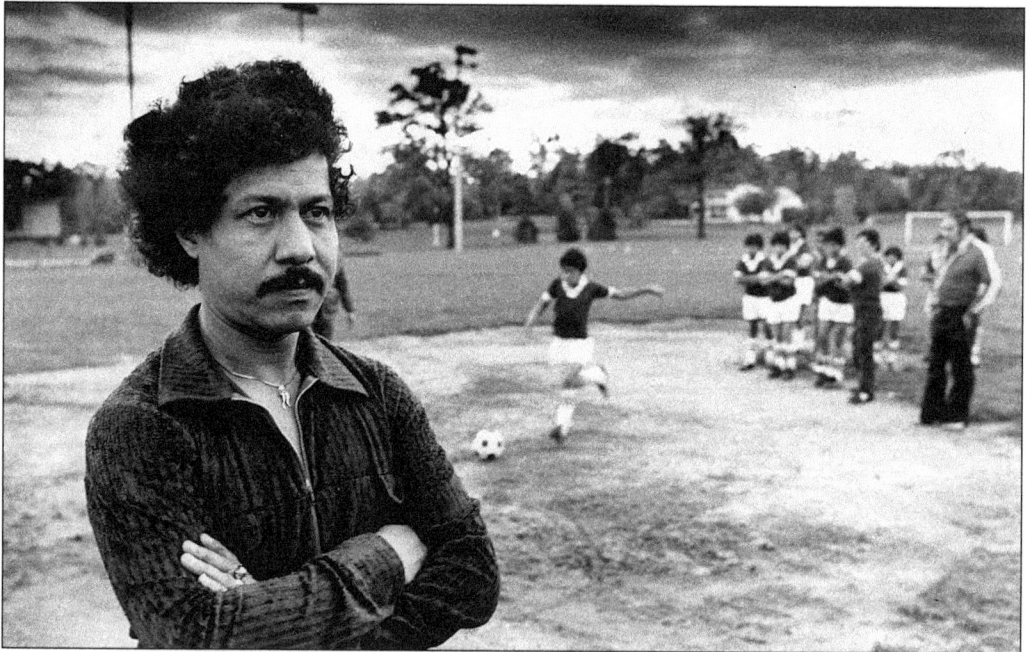

Born in Mexico, José Avilés took a risk coming to Milwaukee, where he eventually entered the plastics industry. In 1987, Avilés took another chance and opened his own plastics fabricating business. Despite a rocky start, his business has grown to be highly respected and successful, proving that some risks are worth taking. (Courtesy of the Milwaukee Journal-Sentinel.)

Thousands of Central Americans fled their countries during the early 1980s, including José Jesús Ocón, who emigrated from Nicaragua to Milwaukee in 1984. Ocón immediately started to work as an automobile mechanic, operating from his own south side backyard. Soon after, he successfully established his own business, which he named Americas Auto Shop.

In 1992, Gov. Tommy Thompson visited the Hispanic Chamber of Commerce of Wisconsin. Those present for a photo oppportunity include board president Pablo Pedraza (left of Thompson, center front) and executive director Wendy Baumann (far right). María Monreal-Cameron (clutching Thompson's arm) later became CEO of the chamber, which moved into a new building at 1021 West National Avenue in 2005.

Apolinar "Polo" Rivera came to Milwaukee in 1980 from Mexico as an immigrant in search of the American dream. After learning to cook at Monreal's El Matador East, he became chef at Taco Loco inside Supermercado El Rey. This 1995 photograph depicts Polo's first restaurant, La Esmeralda, a taquería at Eleventh and Greenfield Streets. Rivera later relocated his successful business to a larger building at 1801 South Eleventh Street.

Ernesto and Heriberto "Beto" Villarreal, brothers from Agualeguas, Nuevo León, Mexico, settled in Milwaukee in the early 1960s. Criselda and Olivia are sisters who are also from the same town as their husbands. The brothers built on the success of their father, Octavio's, small corner grocery store when they opened Supermercado El Rey in 1978 on South Sixteenth Street, now known as César E. Chávez Drive. Astute business people, the Villarreal family built the El Rey empire to include four supermarkets, a tortilla factory, and several smaller outlets around Milwaukee.

Four

RELIGION

Religion is an important part of the lives of all Latino communities. The fact that most Milwaukee Latinos are Catholic and working class means that the church is a central part of community life. In 1926, the Archdiocese of Milwaukee recognized the growing Spanish-speaking community and opened Our Lady of Guadalupe Mission on South Fifth Street. Spanish-speaking priests initially came from Mexico and Spain. As the Puerto Rican community developed in the near northeast side, many attended St. Francis of Assisi Parish and Old St. Mary Parish.

Latinos often have two religious realities: the formal or institutional and the informal or personal. Many Mexicans and Puerto Ricans who never enter a church have, nevertheless, strong faith. They build home altars devoted to the Virgin of Guadalupe. Numerous south side houses are adorned with *nichos*, or shrines devoted to the Virgin.

Religion of the folk variety is seen in the *botánicas* (pharmacies) selling potions, spices, and other articles needed to solve various ailments. These folk remedies provide solace and are a tradition that dates back to the indigenous populations of the Americas. The religious influence is apparent during the community's celebrations surrounding El Día de Los Muertos (Day of the Dead or All Saints' Day) and the Catholic mass during Mexican Fiesta.

In the 1960s, church leaders played an important role in supporting efforts by Latino activists to improve the social conditions of the Spanish-speaking population. Priests and other religious officials advocated for improvements in social services, sometimes helping to create social service agencies. Protestant and Catholic activists pushed for community centers to address poverty and educational deficiencies.

Most recently, south side parish priests and Protestant clergy have spoken out against gang activity and crime, and in favor of civil rights for immigrants. Churches continue to be at the center of providing social services to the Latino community. These services include initiatives to help stem crime and violence and to provide activities for adults and children. Other social services include the provision of legal advice and programs to increase Latino home ownership.

With Archbishop Sebastian Messmer and Fr. Ernesto Osorio Aguirre presiding, Our Lady of Guadalupe Mission was inaugurated on December 12, 1926, at 313 Grove Street (now 719 South Fifth Street).

Nine different Mercedarian priests served at Our Lady of Guadalupe Mission, including Fr. Fidel de la Fuente Santamaría, from Spain, pictured in this 1938 photograph with the students of his catechism class. Father de la Fuente, pastor from September 1937 to March 1944, later ministered in the Diocese of Ponce, Puerto Rico, where he died in 1961.

As a youth, Mexico-born Ernesto Osorio Aguirre and his parents fled as political refugees and settled in Chile. He graduated from both the national and Catholic universities of Chile and practiced medicine for two years before studying theology and being ordained a priest. Osorio returned to Mexico in 1925 but quickly fled again due to the government's violent oppression of the Catholic Church. In 1926, the archbishop of Milwaukee, Sebastian Gebhard Messmer, appointed Father Osorio as "Pastor of all Mexicans and Spanish speaking people of the Archdiocese." Father Osorio celebrated Mass every Sunday in the school hall of Holy Trinity Parish before the Our Lady of Guadalupe Mission for Mexican Catholics was inaugurated on December 12, 1926. Pictured in this June 1927 photograph, standing from left to right at the entrance to the mission, are Rafael Avila, Fr. Ernesto Osorio Aguirre, Celedonio Rodríguez, and Frank J. Gross. Father Osorio, who served as pastor of Our Lady of Guadalupe Mission until October 1927, was also a founding member of the Círculo Social de Amigos "Emilio Carranza."

By 1937, thousands of Latinos lived on Milwaukee's near south side, and many Latino children attended the summer program at the Polish House, near South Fifth and Washington Streets. Emery Cárdenas (fourth row, fourth from left) relates that it was "filled with kids of all nationalities ... Polish, German, Greek, Norwegians, and Mexicans." Approximately half the children pictured here are Latinos, along with Padre Fidel de la Fuente from the Guadalupe Mission.

Ever since the arrival of the first Latino immigrants to Milwaukee, the church has played a crucial role in the group's assimilation and success, welcoming newcomers and helping them find employment and housing. The above photograph of a sizeable first communion class was taken in 1939, outside the Our Lady of Guadalupe Mission.

Born in Puerto Rico, María Correa moved to Milwaukee in 1952 at the age of seven. In 1977, she began a career with the United Community Center (UCC), where she still works today, having served four of the UCC's executive directors. In this 1960 photograph, Correa (left) is pictured at her eighth-grade graduation from the Holy Trinity Church school with her sister Carmen and Fr. Stephen Bono.

Milwaukee's earliest Puerto Rican neighborhood formed north of downtown and around Old St. Mary Parish at the corner of Broadway and Kilbourn Avenue. In a diverse neighborhood of Poles, Germans, Italians, and others, Old St. Mary's embraced Spanish-speaking newcomers to its congregation. Mexican Americans Carlos "Charles" and Teresa Gómez, with sons (from left) Carlos Jr., Edward, Daniel, George, and Alfred, illustrate the parish's diverse richness at this 1961 St. John the Baptist celebration.

Alberto Castro was one of the first Mexican settlers in Milwaukee to work for Northwestern Railroad. In 1930, he helped found Sociedad Mutualista Hispano-Azteca, a Latino mutual aid organization, with which he also served as president. He was also a member of the Holy Name Society and a member of the Guadalupanas Society at Our Lady of Guadalupe Church at Third and Washington Streets, where he is pictured in this photograph.

Sergio Ramos and Lydia Díaz, flanked by parents Amelia Figueroa and Angel Díaz, were married on August 17, 1963, by Rev. Gilbert Marrero in a small Baptist church in Milwaukee. The Díaz family, with strong Pentecostal roots, originated from Puerto Rico. Sergio recalled that Milwaukee police were wary of Latino immigrants, and police would sometimes follow the couple to their north side home to verify that it was their residence.

Cursillo weekends, three-day short courses to deepen one's faith, were introduced to the Archdiocese of Milwaukee in 1965 for men, and in 1966 for women. This photograph is believed to be of the second cursillo ever held in the Archdiocese of Milwaukee in 1966. As of October 2005, the archdiocese had conducted 204 cursillos. Among the *cursillistas* are Dolores Gutiérrez, María Lara, Luz Molina, Dolores Ortíz, and Anicacia Rivera.

In 1946, Our Lady of Guadalupe Mission moved to the former Hanover and South Telephone Exchange at Third and Washington Streets and changed its name to Our Lady of Guadalupe Church. The parish merged with Holy Trinity Parish at 613 South Fourth Street on August 28, 1966, and hundreds of parishioners joined in a procession from Our Lady of Guadalupe to Holy Trinity.

The Cursillo Movement, begun in Spain in the 1940s, was introduced to the Catholic Church in the United States in 1957. Pictured in this photograph around 1970 are cursillistas led by Fr. Wilbert "Wilberto" Lanser at St. Francis of Assisi Parish in Milwaukee. Among the many participants are Emilio Coca, Ramón Cruz, Vicente Delgado, Francisco González, Joe González, Prof. Antonio Martínez, Rafael Reyes, Máximo Rodríguez, and Virgilio Ruíz.

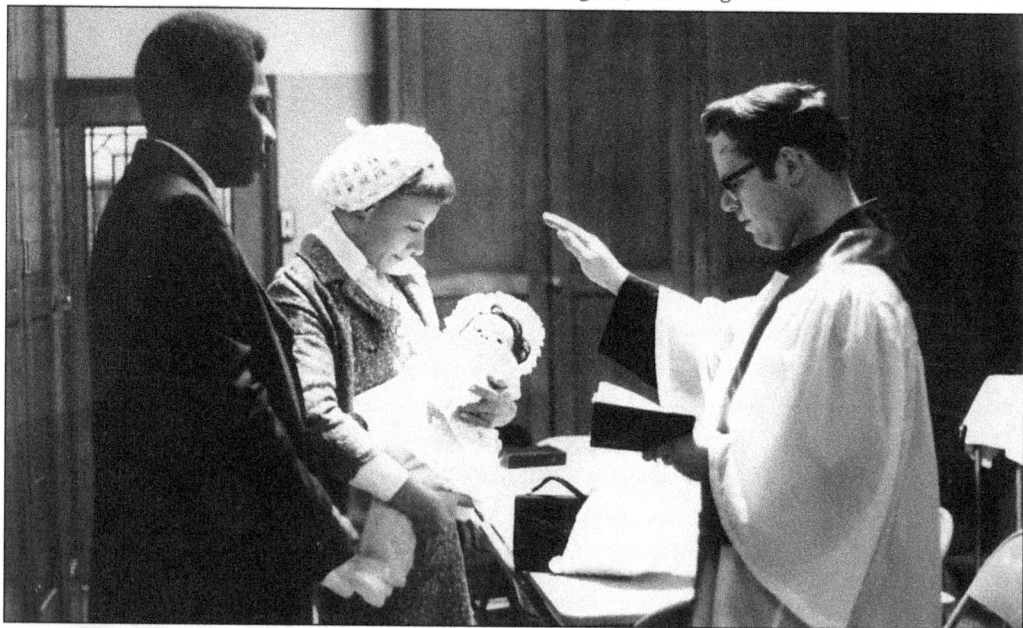

By the late 1950s, St. Francis of Assisi Catholic Church at Fourth and Brown Streets had a significant Latino congregation. As in every Roman Catholic parish in the world, the ritual of pre–Vatican II Masses was celebrated in Latin. Nevertheless, homilies and the day's readings were conducted in Spanish. In this c. 1970 photograph, Fr. Wilbert "Wilberto" Lanser baptizes Edna Rivera in the presence of padrinos José and Cora Quiñónez.

The *quinceañera*, a traditional celebration of a Latina's 15th birthday, recognizes her journey from childhood to maturity and reaffirms religious faith. Many Latino families start saving for the celebration upon the birth of their daughter. In this September 1971 photograph, Neida Burgos of Milwaukee is surrounded by friends and family at her quinceañera at St. Michael Parish. Burgos's third daughter, Adriana, celebrated her own quinceañera in April 2005.

In 1978, Fr. Larry Dulek, associate pastor at St. Joseph Parish in Waukesha, opened the Viernes Santo (Good Friday) procession in front of Strand Food. Ordained in 1973, Father Dulek later led St. Veronica parish and St. Anthony parish in Milwaukee. He founded and directed a pre-seminary program for Latinos, regularly visited the Milwaukee County Jail, and with other clergy formed a campus ministry program at South Division High School.

Originally from San José de Buenaventura, Jalisco, Mexico, Pedro Martínez studied to be a priest for 12 years before realizing that his real vocation was to be married and have a family. In 1980, he married Juanita Bongers, with whom he has had three children. Martínez has served as Archdiocese of Milwaukee director of the Office for Hispanic Ministry since 1983.

Unloading groceries in January 2005, Fr. Eleazar Pérez Rodríguez, pastor of St. Adalbert Parish, was struck by a car driven by a young undocumented Mexican immigrant, and surgeons later amputated his leg. Despite Pérez's plea for leniency, the young man was convicted of hit and run and deported to Mexico. Known for his keen sense of humor, Pérez demonstrates the versatility of his new *pierna computerizada* in November 2005.

Five

CULTURE

Community celebrations, family events, dances, beauty pageants, and musical performances have long been an important part of Milwaukee's Latino culture. Such performances demonstrate the cultural pride Latinos possess and their diverse national origins.

In the early years, Sociedad Mutualista Hispano-Azteca had a drama club that performed Mexican plays and musicals. Parades and parties in the streets and parks celebrated *las fiestas patrias*, or national holidays. Mexicans celebrated Cinco de Mayo (the defeat of the French invaders in Puebla, Mexico, in 1862) and Mexican Independence Day (September 16th). Puerto Ricans celebrated the Grito de Lares commemorating the rebellion against Spanish colonizers in 1868.

During the war years, these celebrations expanded. A Peruvian immigrant, Juan de la Torre, founded the annual Holiday Folk Fair in 1944 that continues celebrating international culture to this day. Anglos and Latinos formed El Club Español de Milwaukee, which held literary and other cultural events pertaining to Latin American and Spanish culture.

As the Puerto Rican population grew following the war, Puerto Ricans played in numerous bands that toured southeastern Wisconsin. The community followed the lead of New York and Chicago in sponsoring a Puerto Rican Day parade. As the celebrations grew larger, organizers moved them to bigger venues. In 1977, Mexican Fiesta moved from the south side to the Maier Festival Park. In the 1990s, the Cinco de Mayo festival moved first to Milwaukee County fairgrounds and then to Mitchell Park. Other festivals were celebrated in Veterans Park and Walker's Square Park.

Latino culture pervades the south side landscape, indicating continued connections to homelands. Murals adorn buildings, marking the Latino community's pride. Houses display statues of the Virgin Mary on the front lawn. Moreover, the south side exhibits evidence of Tex-Mex culture. Some residents wear cowboy boots, and images of cowboy hats adorn cars and store signs. Texas license plates and references to Texas in store names indicate an ongoing cultural connection to the Lone Star State. *Conjunto* bands regularly play in south side clubs.

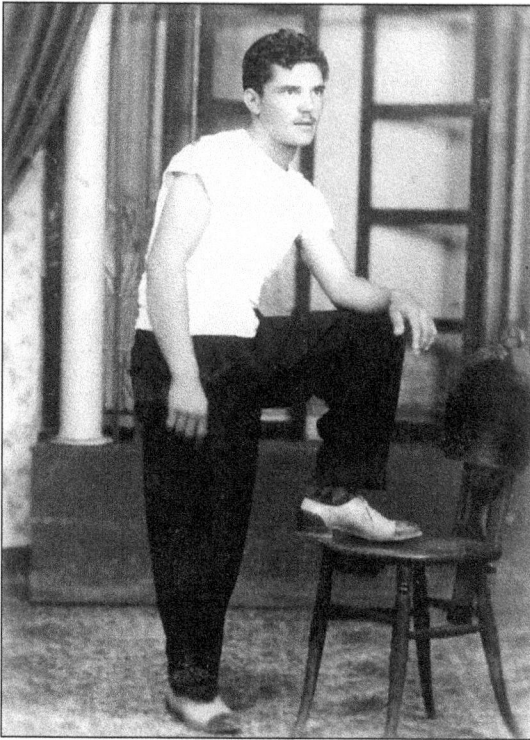

Born in Mexico in 1925, Cruz Ortega (also known locally as Francisco González) worked as a professional dancer until 1969, when he moved to the United States. He raised four children and worked as a chef in numerous Milwaukee restaurants, including El Vagabond, Camino Real, and Piedras Negras. An active member of the UCC Senior Center, Ortega continues to dance and cook recreationally today.

Before Mexican Fiesta became one of the Midwest's largest Latino festivals, there were numerous street festivals held in Milwaukee and surrounding communities. In the mid-1970s, La Casa de Esperanza started Latino Community Days, a street festival held in front of its headquarters on Arcadian Avenue in Waukesha. The festival eventually became Fiesta Waukesha, celebrated annually in Frame Park.

Milwaukee's folkloric group Club Estrellita, active as early as the 1940s, performed in Milwaukee's annual Holiday Folk Fair, Mexican holidays and celebrations, and other events throughout the area. The group was originally comprised of members between the ages of 18 and 30, including Dolores Frías (in white blouse, far right) in this *c.* 1945 photograph.

Sociedad Mutualista Hispano-Azteca sponsored a wide range of activities to the burgeoning Mexican colony in Milwaukee, including concerts, dances, civic events, and other celebrations of special significance to the community's cultural identity. Mexicans and Mexican Americans were particularly interested in the Cinco de Mayo, Día de los Muertos, and Mexican Independence Day celebrations, as evidenced in this 1941 program listing Milwaukee's Mayor Carl Zeidler as presider of the event.

A Peruvian immigrant, Juan de la Torre (center) and his American wife, Ida Mae (left), played a dramatic role in the evolution of Latino culture in Milwaukee. Juan served as president of El Club Español de Milwaukee and cofounded the International Holiday Folk Fair. Ida Mae served as president of the International House Activities Council, chairman of the Folk Fair, and president of the International Institute of Milwaukee.

Spanish-language monthly community newsletter *El Mutualista* was a voice for the Latino community in Milwaukee from 1930 to 1970. The newsletter described news and events, announced upcoming parties, published local poetry, and provided updates on community members who were sick, on vacation, or who had recently died. The July 31, 1949, issue lists Federico Herrera as director and David Valdes as manager.

EL MUTUALISTA

ÓRGANO MENSUAL DE LA S. MUTUALISTA HISPANO-AZTECA.
MILWAUKEE   WISCONSIN

VOL. 3   NO. 7   JULIO 31 DE 1949
DIRECTOR: FEDERICO HERRERA.   GERENTE: DAVID VALDES

**JUSTO HOMENAJE A NUES-
TROS HEROES CAIDOS**

Con la debida reverencia se llevó a cavo una ceremonia póstuma en memoria de los muchachos mexicanos que ofrendaron su sangre y su vida en holocausto a la democracia. Estos soldados méxico-americanos eran residentes de Milwaukee; sus nombres: Hector Cervantes, David Valdes, Salvador Flores y Arturo Quiroz.

La ceremonia consistió en una parada muy lucida, como de dos cuadras de larga y que marchó de la 14 y Nacional a la Tercera y Washington; la formación se componía de un grupo de veteranos con su capellán el Rev. Padre Michael Brown, la banda de los C.W.V., un grupo de la Legión Americana y su banda; la banda de los V.F.W. y la banda de la escuela superior para niñas Mercy; por supuesto que los deudos de los 4 héroes desaparecidos ocupaban lugares prominentes.

Cuando la formación llegó a la iglesia de Nuestra Señora de Guadalupe, se colocó a los deudos de los desaparecidos en una plataforma de honor, especialmente construida; en seguida comenzó la dedicación de un mástil y una bandera

obsequiados por los veteranos de nuestra parroquia, Catholic War Veterans, Post 1279. Algunas personas hablaron y en sus discursos elogiaron el valor, la abnegación y el sacrificio máximo de nuestros muchachos que fueron a la guerra para no volver nunca jamás; entre los oradores prominentes vimos al Sr. Frank Bruce Sr., Mr. Frank L. Greenya, nuestro párroco el Rev. Padre Estanislao, el simpático y amable Padre Julián y el inolvidable Padre Miguelito (father Michael Brown) quien vino a visitarnos desde Carlsbad, N. M..

Hector Cervantes fué representado por sus tios el Sr. Ramón Cervantes y la Sra. Zenona Cervantes; David Valdes Jr. estubo representado por sus papás y hermanas, el Sr. David Valdes Sr., la Sra. Catalina Plancarte de Valdes y las Sritas. Catalina y Carmen Valdes; Arturo Quiroz estubo representado por sus papás el Sr. don Horacio Quiroz y la Sra. Virginia Quiroz; Salvador Flores estubo representado por sus mejores amigos el Sr. Francisco Mariscal y su señora esposa la Sra. Concepción Juárez de Mariscal.

——o——

Mi México lindo, digo con orgullo: a la vez, México lindo, yo soy tuyo

——o——

The International Holiday Folk Fair, an instant success, attracted more than 3,500 visitors to its premiere in December 1944. It remains the nation's largest and oldest ethnic celebration, representing more than 50 ethnic groups and attracting thousands of visitors annually. This image depicts Club Español during an appearance at the fair in its early years.

While band members took a break during a c. 1960 celebration at the South Side Armory at 160 South Sixth Street, their wives picked up instruments to pose for photographs. From left to right are Lupe (wife of Raúl) Correa, Inés (wife of Guadalupe) Macías, Juanita (wife of Pedro) Martínez, Rosa (wife of Frank) Martínez, María (wife of Cruz) Martínez, and Margarita (wife of Ignacio "Nacho") Zaragoza.

Rita Rentería-Valenzuela, daughter of Juanita and Ponciano "Pete" Rentería, grew up on Milwaukee's south side, working in her father's food store. Inspired by her parents' service to the community, she has been active with the Mexican Independence Day parade and, at the time of this book's publication, works for United Migrant Opportunity Services in Milwaukee. She is pictured as prom queen of Don Bosco High School, accompanied by king Tom O'Donnell, in 1962.

Nattily attired in stage costumes, members of the group Los Hermanitos Burgos pose for this 1965 photograph. The band was the first local Latino group to ever perform at Milwaukee Summerfest. Standing from left to right are Héctor Burgos, Elminio Burgos, and Manuel Narváez. Seated are Cecil Negrón (left) and Jesús "Joey" Burgos.

In this 1965 photograph, Grupo Musical José Quiñónez y las Estrellas del Ritmo performs onstage at El Centro Puertorriqueño at 2578 North Richards Street. The band, a regional favorite, regularly performed in Illinois, Indiana, Ohio, and throughout southeast Wisconsin. Numerous bands spent weekends performing for parties, festivals, weddings, and other gatherings. Pictured from left to right are Angel Sánchez, Sebastian Ortíz, José Quiñónez, Isaías Ortíz, Julián Ortíz, and Orlando Narváez.

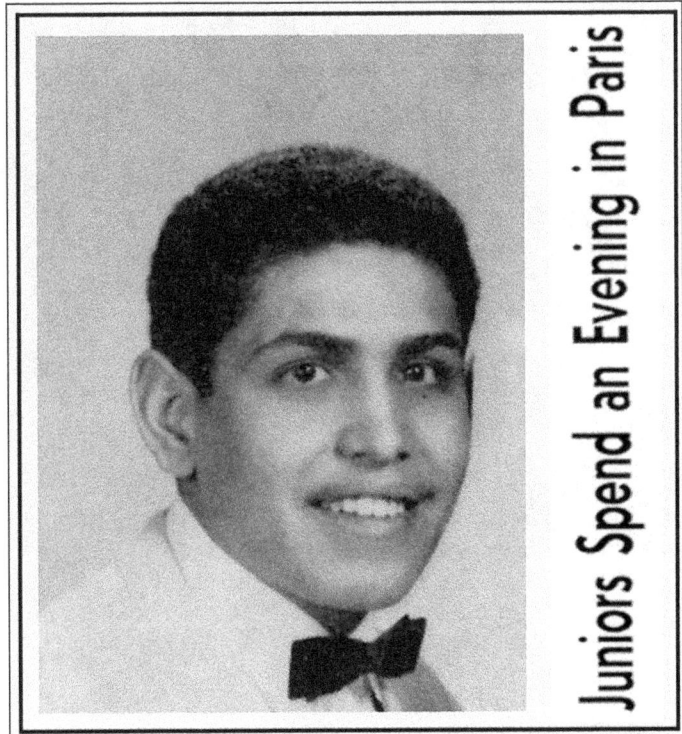

Juniors Spend an Evening in Paris

Racism was still practiced openly in 1966 when Perfecto Rivera, one of the few Latino students at Milwaukee's Pulaski High School, was nominated for king of the junior prom. Several teachers, asserting that Puerto Rico-born Rivera "wouldn't properly represent the student body," wrote Pulaski's principal urging that he be excluded as a candidate. Invited to remove his name from consideration, Rivera politely declined, and Pulaski's students elected him prom king.

This group of youngsters, dressed as ranchers watching a horse race, poses for a photograph while sitting on a rail at the Holiday Folk Fair. From left to right are María Tamargo, unidentified, Zulay Febres Cordero (who at time of publication of this book is the artistic director for Latino Arts, Incorporated), unidentified, Raquel Béjar, and Magda Grijalba.

In the late 1960s and early 1970s, La Orquesta Juvenil performed wherever their adult manager, Enrique Robles, could find them a gig in southeast Wisconsin and the Chicago area. Originally all ranging in age from 12 to 20, band members in this c. 1969 photograph included, from left to right, (kneeling) Victor "Vitín" Narváez, Manuel Narváez, and Alejandro "Ali" Narváez; (standing) Héctor Rodríguez, Félix Colón, María Robles, Luis González, Roberto Dávila, and Walter "Wally" Robles.

In 1948, at age 19, Raúl Correa left his job managing a Piggly Wiggly store in Crystal City, Texas, and came to Milwaukee. Passionate about music, Correa has performed with musical groups in venues all over Milwaukee and southeastern Wisconsin. While his major instrument was always the guitar, he is pictured playing the congas in this 1970 photograph.

Art

Mr. Cole   Mr. Gill

Mr. Poole   Mr. Holt

Mr. Cole, Art department chairman gives a student valuable instruction.

Reynaldo Hernández's interest in art began early, and his body of work features more than 125 murals. Hernández graduated from Milwaukee Boys Tech High School in 1968 and created his first mural by the age of 19. At least 53 Hernández murals exist in Milwaukee, including one that adorns the main building of the United Community Center. Today Hernández is an illustrator and staff artist for WTMJ-TV and owner of Hernández Design Fine Art.

During the 1970s, a number of Milwaukee-area clubs featured Puerto Rican music and dances. La Controversia, formed in 1972, was a notable local band that recorded an album in 1974 named Visión Divina. Through 1977, La Controversia regularly opened for bands such as Fania All Stars, Eddie Palmieri, and others.

Ignacio "Nacho" Zaragoza and his band Orquesta Sensación (featuring the best of Latin and American music) performed together for more than 10 years, until Zaragoza died in a 1973 automobile accident. Members of the group, photographed around 1970, are, from left to right, (first row) Nacho Zaragoza, unidentified, Ernesto Cornejo, and Victor Cabán; (second row) Jesús Zuñiga, Chuck Right, María Violeta Rivera, José Alabarría, John Gardipee, Mike Martínez, Bonnie Cerda, Lupe Macías, and Raúl Correa.

Guadalupe "Lupita" Béjar, then 24 years old, came from Jalisco, Mexico, to Milwaukee in 1969. A longtime activist for human rights, bilingual education, workers' rights, and elderly and other social justice issues, Béjar was named "Citizen of the Year" by the Lawyers' Wives of Greater Milwaukee in 1977. Béjar is also well known as a performer of traditional Mexican folk music and as "Loopy the Clown."

Frank González, born in Milwaukee, is the son of Francisco and Eleuteria (Ruano) González, immigrants from Nochistlán, Zacatecas, Mexico. González served as a board member with Bruce-Guadalupe Community School and the Walker's Point Development Corporation and represented the south side for 17 years as commissioner with the Social Development Commission. This photograph features González dressed as a *charro*, a Mexican cowboy, for the 1972 Mexican Independence Day parade.

Reviving an earlier tradition, Milwaukee has celebrated Mexican Independence Day every year since 1970 with a parade. The annual event, first sponsored by the Council for the Spanish Speaking and the Hispanic Chamber of Commerce, is now sponsored by United Migrant Opportunity Services (UMOS). The parade has utilized a variety of south side routes, including one through West Mitchell Street as shown in this 1973 photograph.

In the 1970s, Dolores Frías (standing, back row) revived the inactive Club Estrellita as a youth organization. The Estrellistas are pictured at a March 7, 1973, performance at WMVS Channel 10 in Milwaukee. When Frías died in 2002, her daughter Silvia (middle row, third from left) assumed leadership of the group for a brief period.

Milwaukee's Latino community hosted Canto al Pueblo, a national Chicano arts festival, from April 28 to May 9, 1977. The festival drew a large collection of artists, musicians, and poets from throughout the Midwest eager to share their work and ideas. Here Francisco Urbina (right) reads to the crowd with musical accompaniment as onlookers take in the events' stimulating atmosphere.

With the popularity of dominoes in the Latino community, the Liga de Dominó del Centro Unido became an important recreational organization. Antonio "Tony" Ithier, top-left in this 1978 photograph, is well known for his leadership role in the league, in which he organized and judged games, kept records of champions, and enforced the rules.

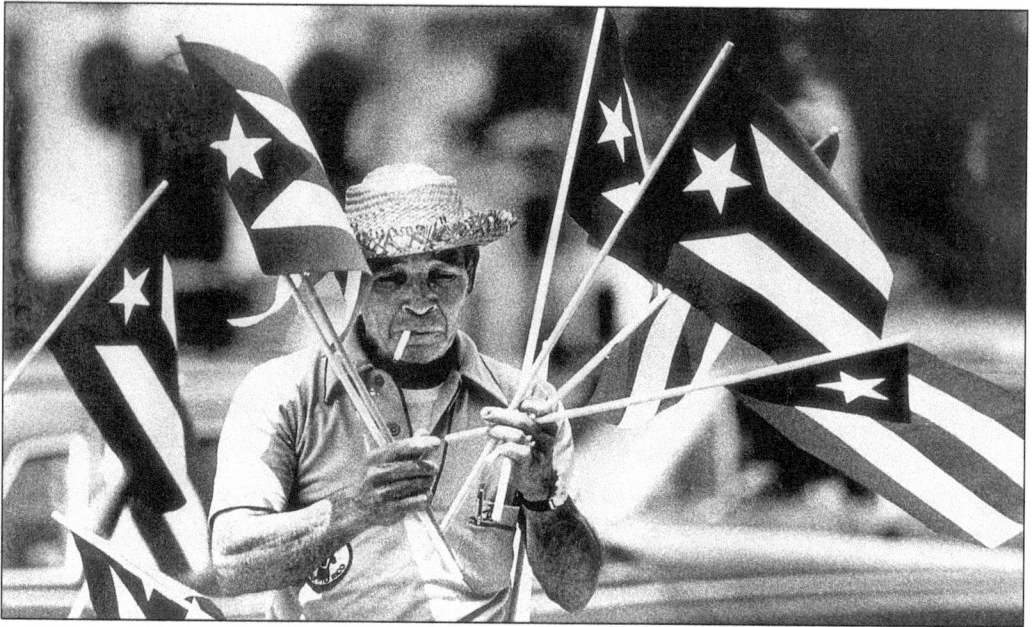

In 1951, local Milwaukee foundries recruited 100 Puerto Rican workers, and by 1953, approximately 4,000 Puerto Ricans had settled in the area, where many found jobs in foundries, tanneries, and manufacturing plants. In this 1978 photograph, Joseph González sells Puerto Rican flags at the Juneau Park party after the annual Puerto Rican parade. By that time, almost 20,000 Puerto Ricans were living in the Milwaukee area. (Courtesy of the Milwaukee Journal-Sentinel.)

In 1979, parade organizer Mariano Avilés portrayed John the Baptist, Puerto Rico's patron saint, in Milwaukee's San Juan Bautista parade. Born in Mayagüez, Puerto Rico, Avilés has called Milwaukee home since 1953. Active in Latino community building since the early 1960s, Avilés has also proudly defended civil and workers' rights, personally and as a union counselor with United Steel Workers Local 1610.

Puerto Ricans in Milwaukee, understandably proud of their heritage, love a parade. On June 23, 1979, an unseasonably cool day with a high of just 57 degrees, parade watchers gathered at Kilbourn Park, bundled up in jackets to celebrate the feast day of San Juan Bautista, patron saint of Puerto Rico. Hairstyles and fashions provide evidence that the "Disco Era" was still very much alive in Milwaukee.

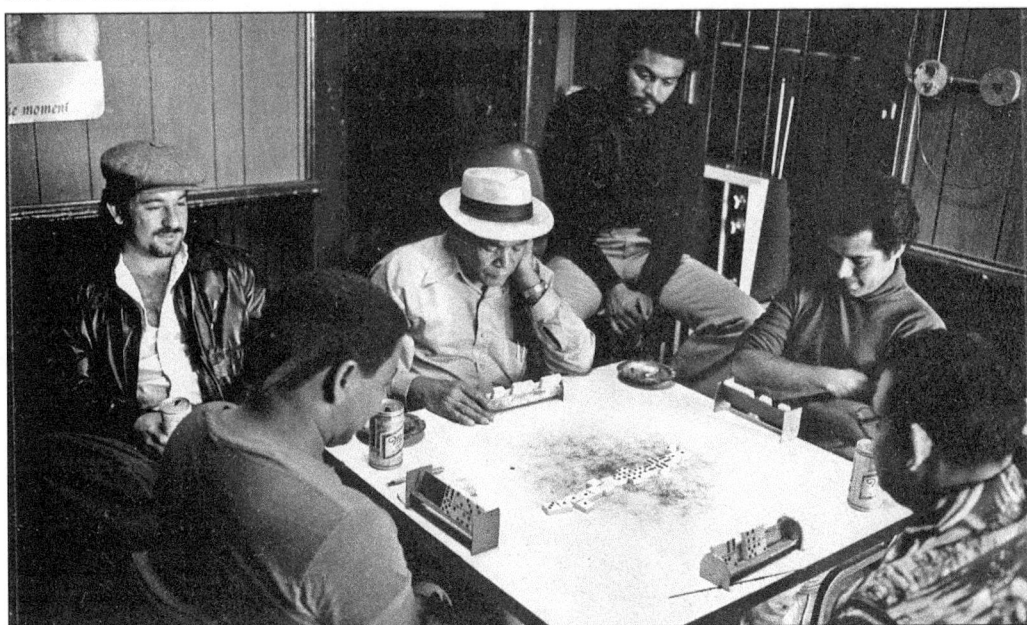

Played all over in parks, taverns, and homes, dominoes is a very popular pastime in many Latin American countries, especially those of the Caribbean. With the immigration of many Latinos to Milwaukee, the pastime has continued on as an important part of local Latino culture. This 1980 Robert Glick photograph was taken during a dominoes tournament at the Juana Díaz Tavern on South Sixth Street in Milwaukee.

Felipe Rodríguez's Andando Solo performed at almost all of the Mexican and Puerto Rican parades and celebrations. In this 1980 Robert Glick photograph, Rodríguez teams up with other local musical talent to perform at the Guadalupe Center school festival.

In this early 1980s photograph, the Puerto Rican Festivals Committee honors volunteers in appreciation for their contributions in organizing the Puerto Rican parade. From left to right are Elsa Aponte, Sonia Martínez, Jertha Ramos, Myrna Gómez, Oscar Ramos, Jorge Arcelay, and Virginia García.

Félix González left Mexico as a single man to come to Milwaukee in 1927, where he married. González was active in the Círculo Social de Amigos "Emilio Carranza," and later in Sociedad Mutualista Hispano-Azteca, which for approximately 40 years provided recreational activities, cultural events, and burial assistance. This 1980 Robert Glick photograph shows Félix and his wife, Aurora González, outside the couple's home on West Cherry Street.

Music is a vital part of any successful festival, and over the years, Patricia Zaragoza de Barboza has helped make many local festivals a success. A popular local singer who volunteered her talent to entertain the crowds, she is pictured in mariachi costume with her husband, Luís Barboza, at the 1984 Mexican Independence Day festival. Today Luís Barboza is recognized as a prominent architect.

Long before she ever became an attorney and assistant family court commissioner in Milwaukee County, Ana Berrios was one of the queens of the 1986 Puerto Rican Parade. From left to right are Ana Berrios, Annete Alvarado, and Hortensia Sánchez.

With humble beginnings in 1975 as a celebration on Milwaukee's south side, Mexican Fiesta has grown to be a wildly popular annual event on the Summerfest Grounds. The festival raises funds to provide scholarships for area Latino students and to maintain and increase awareness of Mexican and Latino cultures. This 1987 photograph shows a crowd enjoying a popular mariachi band's performance at the Summerfest Grounds' Miller Jazz Oasis.

Held during the last weekend of August, Milwaukee Mexican Fiesta traditionally conducts a Sunday morning Mass at the Marcus Amphitheater. Hundreds of believers join clergy, Knights of Columbus, pageant queens, choirs, and mariachi musicians in a procession from the festival grounds to the amphitheater, as pictured in this 1990s photograph.

The Puerto Rican Festivals Committee held its fourth-annual fashion show and banquet as part of the June 1990 celebration. The 14 lovely models in this photograph of the fashion show titled "Attitudes" demonstrate their timeless Latina attitude while displaying the hottest styles at the start of the last decade of the millennium.

Michael Reyes, of Puerto Rican descent, is well known in the Milwaukee area as an advocate for, and expert on, Latin music. Reyes (third from left) is shown in 1992 with, from left to right, Mayor John Norquist, Ricardo Díaz (then executive director of the Housing Authority of the City of Milwaukee), and the legendary Tito Puente, who was in Milwaukee for a performance, which Reyes had helped arrange. In 2006, Reyes was elected president of Latino Arts, Incorporated.

The Esperanza Unida International Building at 611 West National Avenue showcases a mural designed by Latino muralist Reynaldo Hernández. A defining symbol of peace and diversity in the community, the mural consists of 285 aluminum panels and stretches 60 feet high and 152 feet wide. In crafting the mural, Hernández worked with local youth apprentices. Installed in 1993 and restored in 1999 following a violent windstorm, this is Wisconsin's largest mural.

There are many examples of Latino public art in Milwaukee's near south side, including Robert Cisneros's *History of Latinos in Milwaukee* mural at Ninth and Mineral Streets, on the north wall of the Bruce-Guadalupe Community School. Cisneros, a well-known artist in Milwaukee, dedicated the work on October 12, 1995. Unfortunately, several notable murals from the 1970s have not survived, including one on the south wall of the UCC, which was covered when an addition was constructed in 1997. Zulay Febres-Cordero Oszkay, artistic director of Latino Arts, Incorporated, designed the nearby shrine to la Virgen de Guadalupe at South Ninth and Washington Streets, featuring a statue by sculptor Alejandro Romero.

Organized and created by Cecil Negrón and Michael Reyes, the group Bembe Orchestra poses backstage at Summerfest in 1993. Pictured from left to right are (standing) Tony ?, Walter Robles, José Morales, Scott ?, Vince Fuh, Angel Luís Sánchez, Luís Díaz, Esteban Alayeto, Aleja Narváez, José Santaella, David Bayless, Mike Betz, Carlos "Quinto" Eguis, Dr. Claude Calliet, Rollo Amstead, Orlando Cabrera, Edgar Martínez, Tom Washatka, Michael Franchesi, Julie Wood, Victor Narváez, Bob ?, Octavio Rivera Jr., and Albert Rivera; (seated and kneeling) Manuel Narváez, Toty Ramos, Cecilio "Papa" Negrón Jr., Ramón Vélez (behind Cecilio), Mingo Burgos, Orlando Sánchez, Sergio "Veneno" Poventud, and Neal Chandek.

Six

SPORTS

Sports help bring people together and serve as a focus of social activity, and when people face barriers to employment promotion, sports provide an outlet. The Latino community valued and supported athletic competition. Numerous Latinos have played on city high school football, basketball, and track teams. Latino youth have succeeded in high school and amateur sports, which serve to reinforce positive values such as the importance of teamwork, individual effort, and self-worth.

Boxing has long been an especially popular activity, with boxing gymnasiums on the city's south side attracting hopeful champions and matches bringing out large audiences to cheer their favorite contenders. Boxing has a strong history and tradition in Mexico and the rest of Latin America. Milwaukee is home to Israel "Shorty" Acosta, who would have participated in the 1980 Summer Olympics had Pres. Jimmy Carter not boycotted the games in response to the USSR's invasion of Afghanistan. Acosta has developed numerous champions from the UCC gymnasium and has gone on to coach other Olympic boxers.

Similarly, many Latinos bowled and played soccer and baseball in Milwaukee. Bowling teams sponsored by south side taverns toured the state in the 1950s and competed against other Latino teams. Soccer and baseball have strong Latin American traditions. Pickup soccer matches are seen throughout the city, with Latinos of every nationality competing. South side soccer leagues are now community social events. In the 1950s, Puerto Rican Félix Mantilla played for the Milwaukee Braves. In his honor, the community formed a Little League baseball association that continues today.

At the UCC, César Pabón was long a fixture in the recreation program. In his younger days, Pabón was a well-known professional wrestler who was featured as "El Superman" on Puerto Rican television. Pabón came to Milwaukee in 1968 and began working at the UCC, known in those days as The Spot. He built a boxing ring, put up basketball hoops, and organized neighborhood youth into boxing, wrestling, weight lifting, and basketball programs. Pabón worked at the UCC until his retirement in 2004.

Brought to Milwaukee in 1914 by promoter George Ryan, Mexican boxer Frank Grace fought professionally for more than 20 years and won a number of championships. After retiring from the ring, Grace opened a pool hall in the neighborhood of Kinnickinnic and Lincoln Avenues and operated a downtown window-washing business. This c. 1917 photograph shows the lean Grace in top fighting condition.

In the summer of 1940, Boric's Club Mexico sponsored a baseball team in Milwaukee's municipal Double-A League. In its inaugural season, George Robles hit over .300, and the team's star pitcher, Tony Cuéllar, pitched a no-hitter but broke his leg sliding into second base in the very next game. The team finished the season in fourth place. With America's involvement in World War II looming, the team had disbanded by 1941.

George Robles was born in Texas in 1913. In 1926, his family settled in Milwaukee, where his father, John Robles, worked in packing houses and the railroad. When he graduated from Bay View High School in 1932, George was the school's first-ever Latino graduate. He later worked at a tannery, as a machinist with Kearney and Trecker, and with Oilgear before retiring in 1976. In 1975, George cofounded and served as first executive director of La Guadalupana Senior Center at 800 South Fifth Street. A longtime community activist and dedicated volunteer, George earned numerous awards before passing away in January 2005. In this 1931 photograph, he wears the football uniform of Bay View High School, complete with leather helmet.

Following World War II, bowling was a popular form of recreation on Milwaukee's south side. Although many aspects of society were not yet integrated, bowling crossed color lines in the ethnically diverse neighborhood. In this late-1940s photograph, Silviano Hernández (at right) and friends meet at Greenfield Arcade, a popular bowling alley near Sixth Street and Greenfield Avenue.

Carlos "Charley" Sandoval opened one of the first south side taverns that catered to Latino immigrants. Milwaukee Latinos enjoyed bowling, so Sandoval's business sponsored a bowling team, whose members pose in front of the Mexico Inn, located at 633 South Fifth Street, around 1941. In the windows are unidentified, Joe Sánchez, Carmello Patti, Henry Ríos, and Lupe Marmolejo. Standing, center, is George Robles, with Sandoval in the doorway.

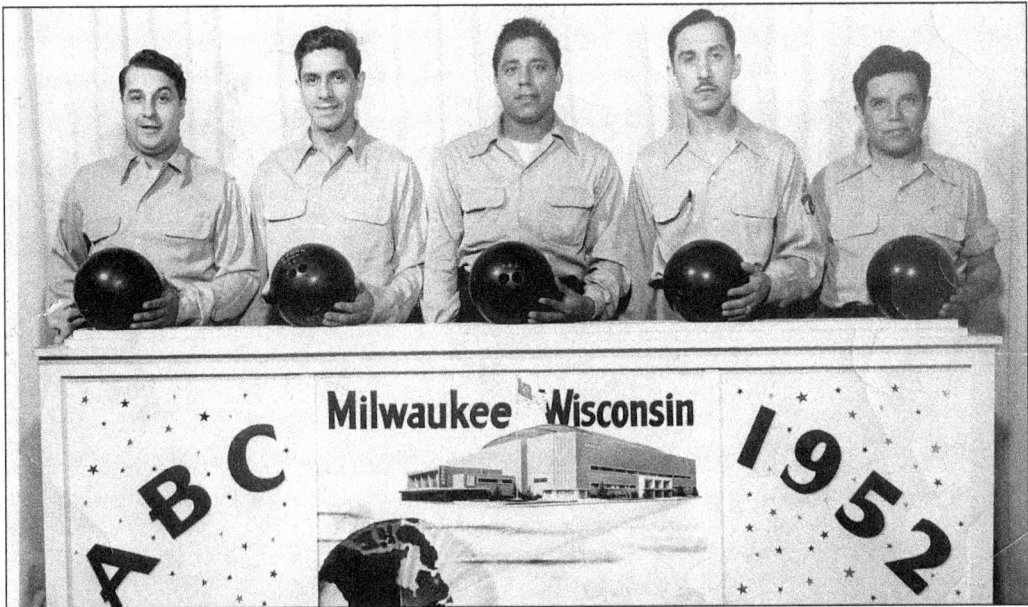

Until 1950, the American Bowling Congress (ABC), headquartered in the Milwaukee area, restricted its membership exclusively to white males. Pressured by legal challenges, the ABC finally changed its constitution, opening membership to minorities. In 1952, the Milwaukee Arena hosted the ABC Championships Tournament, and the team sponsored by the Mexico Inn competed. From left to right are Ilarión Arenas, Joseph Sánchez, George Robles, Baudalio "Buddy" Rodríguez, and Lupe Rentería.

The 1950s social life for Milwaukee Latinos often revolved around Catholic parishes that regularly sponsored social events, dances, picnics, the Catholic Youth Organization (CYO), and sports leagues. The Holy Ghost Dartball Tournament took place in April 1957 at Our Lady of Guadalupe Church at Third and Washington Streets. Pictured from left to right are (first row) Armando Villarreal, Aurelio Granado, Francisco Figueroa, Federico Herrera, and Félix Gómez; (second row) Adolfo Herrera, Valentín Figueroa, Antonio Gómez, Juan Ambriz, Juan Matos, and Daniel Camacho.

During the 1960s, many Latino youth played soccer in a CYO league sponsored by the Archdiocese of Milwaukee. This 1962 photograph of the team from Milwaukee's Old St. Mary Parish (at right), coached by Jorge Sánchez, poses with the team from Our Lady of Lourdes Parish before a game at Washington Park.

Between 1967 and 1979, Milwaukee Boys Tech won 10 city of Milwaukee and five Wisconsin state high school wrestling championships. In 1968, Héctor Cruz and Mike Morales each won individual state championships, helping earn the Boys Tech team second place overall. Pictured in 1967, from left to right, are grapplers Mark Morales, Héctor Cruz, Michael Morales, and Steve Gorecki.

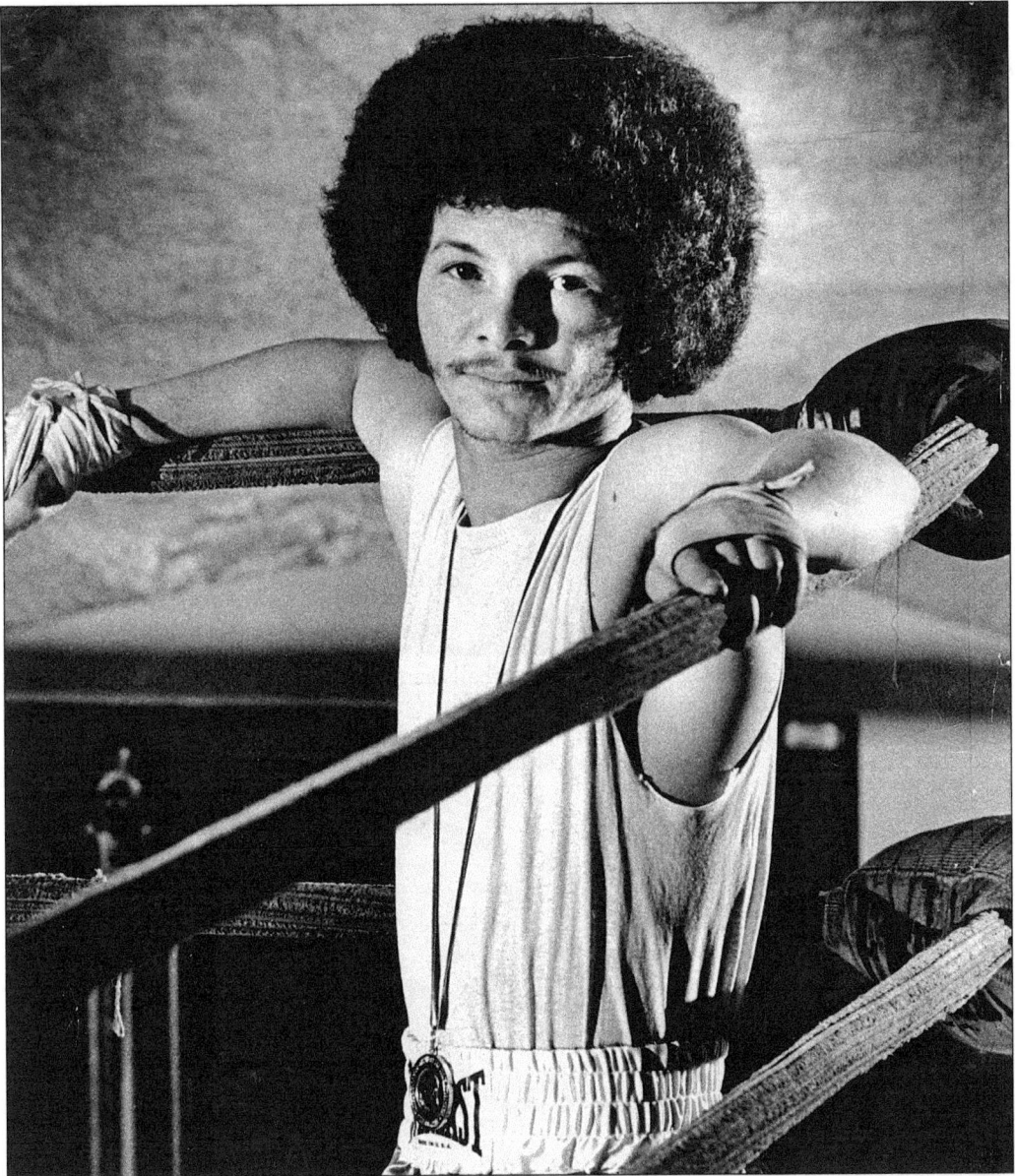

Israel "Shorty" Acosta left Maunabo, Puerto Rico, at the age of 17 and soon met Cuban-born Miguel Lassus, who was training boxers at the UCC's gymnasium. Fighting at 106 pounds, Acosta went on to win more than 500 bouts, lost only 16, and was the U.S. National Men's Champion in 1977. A strong favorite to win the gold medal in the 1980 Moscow Olympics, Acosta's dream was derailed when the U.S. boycotted the games in protest of the Soviet Union's invasion of Afghanistan. Determined to make the 1984 Olympic team and compete in Los Angeles, at age 31, Acosta reported for the box-offs as the oldest participant in the competition. In the final fight of his amateur career, Acosta lost a narrow 3-2 decision to Paul González. Many, including Acosta, felt that he had beaten González, the eventual Olympic gold medalist. Acosta joined the U.S. boxing team at the 2000 Olympics in Sydney, Australia, as an assistant coach. Shorty is pictured in this remarkable c. 1980 photograph sporting his famous Afro haircut. (Courtesy of the Milwaukee Journal-Sentinel.)

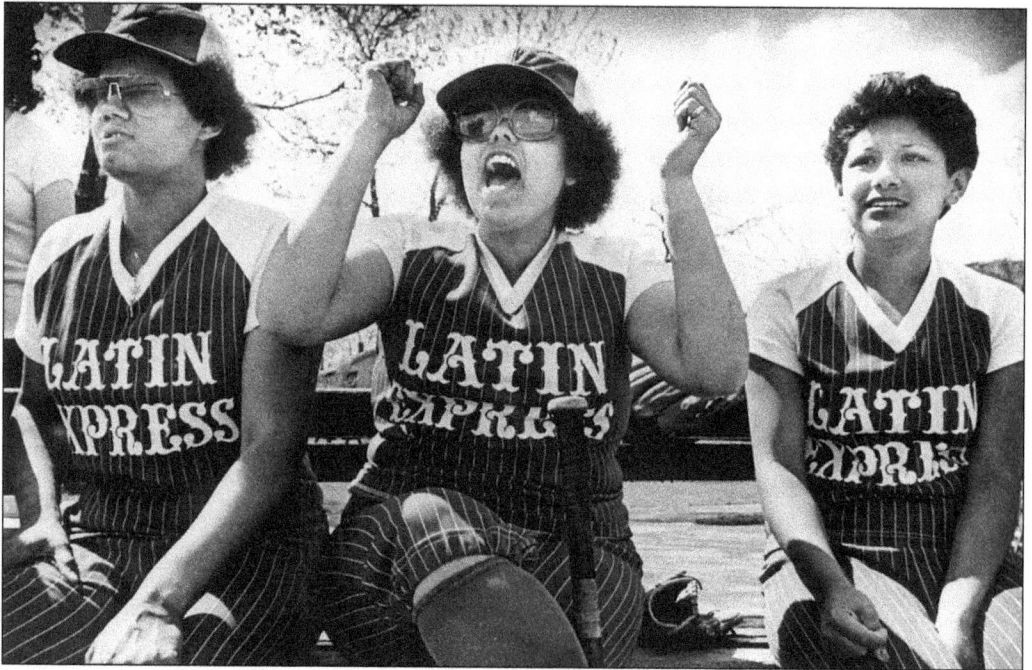

In the late 1970s, the Latin Express women's softball team won several championships. Named after its sponsor, a Latin American musical group, the team played for five years on south side softball diamonds. During a 1975 game in Baran Park, from left to right, are Silvia Zapata, Clara Gaud, and an unidentified woman. (Courtesy of the Milwaukee Journal-Sentinel.)

Although baseball is a distant second to soccer (*fútbol*), Latinos have complemented major-league rosters as early as 1871, playing a significant role in the American national pastime. This 1986 El Universal photograph by accomplished photojournalist Rafael Fernández shows Milwaukee Brewers players Teddy Higuera (Mexico), Juan Castillo (Dominican Republic), Jaime Cocanower (Puerto Rico), Ben Oglivie (Panama), and Juan Nieves (Puerto Rico), along with Dr. Daniel Valdéz and Duamel Vellon (front).

In 1990, the Selección Latina de Fútbol de Wisconsin, the state's all-star Latino soccer team, won the Torneo de Ligas del Medio-Oeste, the Midwest's Latino soccer championship. José Avilés (front left) sponsored and coached the team. Avilés invited Antonio Carbajal (back, with glasses) to be his personal guest. Carbajal, popularly known as "El Cinco Copas," played in five consecutive World Cup tournaments as goalie for the Mexican national team.

As a coach, Israel "Shorty" Acosta has developed many outstanding amateur boxers, including 1980 junior national champion Rogelio Cabral, two-time national champion LeChaunce Shepherd, and 1998 Goodwill Games gold medalist Teaunce Shepherd. In 1993, the cover of *Boxing USA* magazine pictured Acosta with Héctor Colón, 1993 U.S. Welterweight/147 pounds champion. Colón earned seven titles in seven different weight classes while training under Acosta in the UCC boxing program.

79

Félix "The Cat" Mantilla, born in Puerto Rico, played for the Milwaukee Braves from 1956 to 1961. The Félix Mantilla Little League, begun by the UCC in 1975, continues today aided by local sponsors. The Félix Mantilla All-Stars team poses outside the UCC in 1993 with, from left to right, Humberto Alonso from McDonald's, Lupe Martínez from UMOS, Oscar Cervera from Mexican Fiesta, and coach Emilío López.

Before César "El Superman" Pabón came to Milwaukee from Puerto Rico in the late 1960s, he had a popular television wrestling program. Pabón, with a great deal of experience working with teenagers, became associate director of the UCC and developed a successful athletic program. In 2003, the UCC inaugurated the César Pabón Fitness Center in honor of Pabón, who retired in 2004.

Seven

MEDIA

Milwaukee's Latino community, like the city's other ethnic populations, has always sought ways to express its views, defend its culture, use the mother tongue, and exchange information and news about the homeland. The city's earliest Latino newspapers dated from the 1920s. These included *Boletín Informativo* and *Sancho Panza*. From 1930 to 1970, the Mexican social organization Sociedad Mutualista Hispano-Azteca published a newspaper, *El Mutualista*, that featured community news, social reporting, and poetry. In the late 1960s and early 1970s, *La Guardia*, a south side newspaper founded by Chicano and Puerto Rican activists, covered the fight for Latino civil rights. In 1975, the *Milwaukee Journal* hired John M. Torres to write the column Latin Corner. In 1982, the paper hired Carolina García to cover Milwaukee's Latino community, and she rose to become assistant managing editor.

Later Latinos published magazines and produced radio and television programs, providing Latinos a chance to exchange information, celebrate successes, and criticize discrimination. These media also helped publicize Latino businesses, provide experience leading to employment in communication fields, and cover events that did not receive adequate coverage by the mainstream media.

The first Spanish radio program began in 1949 when Dante Navarro hosted *La Hora Hispana* (*The Hispanic Hour*) on WFOX; it ran until 1982. By the 1970s, Latinos hosted radio programs featuring salsa music and other cultural programming. In the 1970s, Milwaukee Public Television (MPTV) began airing *Panorama Hispano*, a television show featuring interviews of Latinos in business, the public schools, and nationally known Latino figures. Cuban American Raúl Galván began making public television programming in the 1970s and today is the production manager at MPTV. In the 1990s, Tony Báez moderated another public television show in which he interviewed prominent members of Milwaukee's Latino community.

By the 1990s, the Latino community supported several weekly newspapers, including the *Latino Community News*, *Spanish Times*, *Spanish Journal*, and *El Conquistador*. All included articles and advertising in both Spanish and English, and all published news not readily available in the mainstream press. Most recently, the *Milwaukee Journal-Sentinel* has launched *¡Aquí! Milwaukee*, a glossy semimonthly magazine focusing on local Latino issues, personalities, and events.

As a young man looking for adventure, Dante Navarro left Mexico in 1945. Upon settling in Milwaukee, he was frustrated at being unable to find any Spanish-language radio programs, so in 1949, he started the first such program on WFOX (now known as WNOV 960 AM.) His widely popular program, *La Hora Hispana*, ran until 1982, an uninterrupted stretch of 33 years.

La Guardia was the first modern-day bilingual newspaper in Milwaukee, addressing the Latino community. Founded in 1969, the newspaper clearly had an agenda to fuel grassroots organizing for social and political change. Created by Roberto Hernández, Avelardo "Lalo" Valdéz, Juan Alvarez Cuauhtémoc, Ernesto Chacón, and others, *La Guardia* was critical to the local Latino civil rights movement.

Yolanda Ayubi came to Milwaukee from Colombia in the early 1970s and, as president and coordinator of the Hispanic Coalition (Coalición Hispana), worked tirelessly on behalf of the rights of Latinos. Her contribution was instrumental in beginning the production of *Panorama Hispano,* the first Spanish-language television show in the city, on MPTV. Ayubi is pictured here, at right, on the show's set. (Courtesy of the Milwaukee Journal-Sentinel.)

During the 1970s, there were more than two dozen Spanish-language radio and television programs airing in southeastern Wisconsin, including *Cantares de México* with Rudy Sandoval, *Corazón Latino* with Dante Navarro, *Impactos Musicales* with Iluminado González, *La Voz de la Raza* with Rigo Hernández, and *Salsa y Bembé* with Héctor Pérez. Many programs, including *Asi Es Mi Tierra* with Carlos Gamiño, were promoted with window posters in Latino businesses and agencies.

ASI ES MI TIERRA
PROGRAMA CULTURAL LATINO
EMISORA UNIVERSITARIA WUWM 89.7 FM
Presenta Musica Continua, Historia, Noticias
y Comentarios de Actualidad
LES BRINDA LO MAS IMPORTANTE DE SU CULTURA
Que es su Historia, su Costumbre y su Música
★ SABADOS ★
DE 9:00 A 11:30 A. M.
DIRECTOR Y LOCUTOR
CARLOS GAMIÑO
SALUD LATINOS
Y LA GLORIA POR SERLO
Cortesia de Casa MARTINEZ, VELAZQUEZ Discount Store y ARECIBEÑA Record Shop
J. & O. Printing   1326 W. Cullerton   Chicago, Illinois   Tel. 243-5577

83

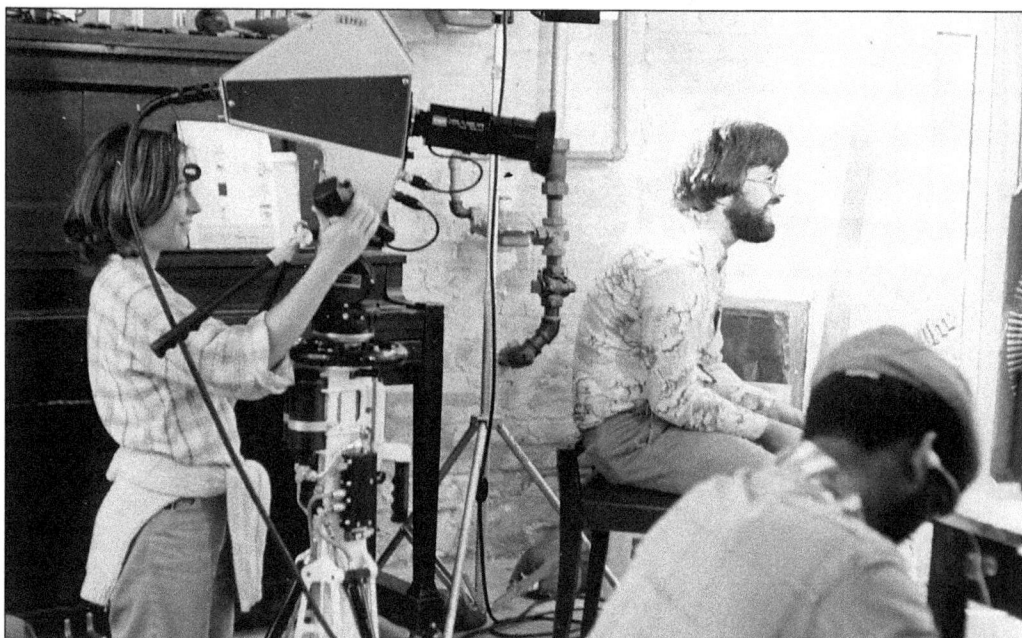

Raúl Galván, born in Cuba, left the island in 1961. Galván began a career in television production in 1973 and by 1975 was the youngest producer/director at MPTV. He has produced and directed *Panorama Hispano*, *Para Usted*, and numerous documentaries and sporting events. Galván, top right in this 1975 photograph, has won numerous awards and currently is manager of program productions at MPTV.

John M. Torres, pioneer Latino broadcaster and writer, began his career in the early 1970s with Milwaukee radio station WNOV-AM. In 1975, Torres became the *Milwaukee Journal's* first Latino writer with the weekly column Latin Corner. The first Latino reporter at WISN-TV, he later founded television station WDJT-TV. Torres served as an editor of *La Guardia*, Milwaukee's first modern-day bilingual newspaper, and as the Latino Press Club of Wisconsin's first president.

Milwaukee-based magazine *Variedades: La Revista Hispana del Medio-Oeste.* presented professional-quality photographs and well-written articles about the arts, fashion, politics, and people of interest. Published quarterly and written almost entirely in Spanish, *Variedades* was probably ahead of its time. The magazine folded in 1979 after publishing its second issue, pictured here.

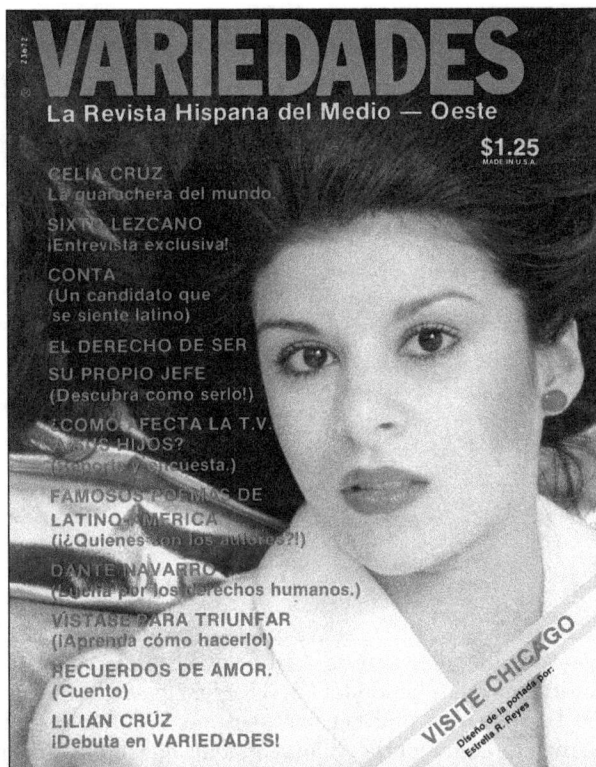

VARIEDADES
La Revista Hispana del Medio — Oeste

$1.25
MADE IN U.S.A.

CELIA CRUZ
La guarachera del mundo.

SIXTO LEZCANO
¡Entrevista exclusiva!

CONTA
(Un candidato que
se siente latino)

EL DERECHO DE SER
SU PROPIO JEFE
(¡Descubra cómo serlo!)

¿CÓMO AFECTA LA T.V.
A SUS HIJOS?
(Señores, encuesta.)

FAMOSOS POETAS DE
LATINO AMÉRICA
(¡¿Quienes son los autores?!)

DANTE NAVARRO
(Lucha por los derechos humanos.)

VÍSTASE PARA TRIUNFAR
(¡Aprenda cómo hacerlo!)

RECUERDOS DE AMOR.
(Cuento)

LILIÁN CRÚZ
¡Debuta en VARIEDADES!

VISITE CHICAGO

Diseño de la portada por:
Estrella R. Reyes

Victor Huyke, self-proclaimed "King of Weekly Newspapers," was born in Puerto Rico but grew up in Milwaukee. In July 1998, Huyke founded *El Conquistador*, widely respected today as a primary news source for Milwaukee's Latino community. Huyke (right) is pictured in an earlier year with Carlos Romero Barceló, former governor of Puerto Rico and resident commissioner for the U.S. House of Representatives.

Carolina García is one of America's most successful Latina journalists. A grant writer for the Latin American Union for Civil Rights, in 1982, she joined the *Milwaukee Journal* as a columnist on Latino issues and became assistant and Sunday editor. In 1995, she was named assistant managing editor for the *Milwaukee Journal-Sentinel*. As a journalist, García led national endeavors to advance hiring and promotion of minorities and women in the nation's newsrooms.

As hostess for the Spanish radio program *Raquel Con Usted*, a musical show featuring the rhythms of many Spanish-speaking nations, Raquel Del Toro became a well-known personality and treasured member of the community. She has served as a volunteer for various Milwaukee-area Latino organizations for more than 20 years. She is pictured at Fiesta Waukesha in 1986, interviewing Anselmo Villarreal, executive director of La Casa de Esperanza.

The early 1970s marked the beginning of a series of programs related to Latino community affairs produced by MPTV. In 1974, *Panorama Hispano* was broadcast on Channel 10, hosted by Angel Rivera, Yolanda Ayubi, and José Quiñónes. In early 1976, Raúl Galván began producing *Para Usted*, and in 1987, Armando Bras and Joe Ochoa (pictured at the program's set, from left to right) launched the *Conciencia* series.

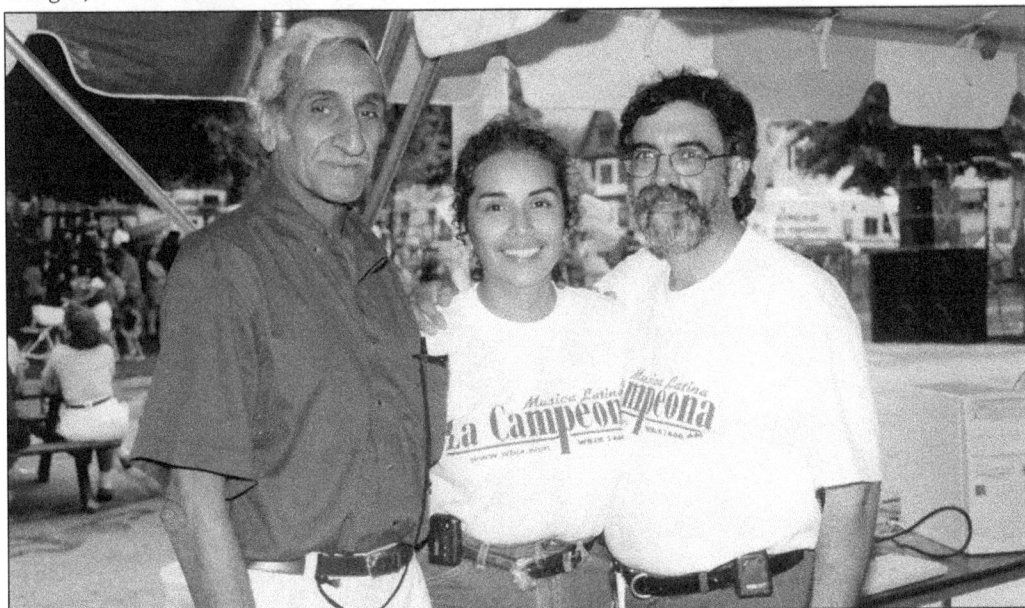

Born in Uruguay, Tony Kalil (left) is the editor and publisher of the *Spanish Times* weekly newspaper, which he founded in September 1988. The newspaper has grown to be widely acclaimed as an influential voice in Milwaukee's Latino community. Kalil is pictured during a UCC fiesta, with Patricia Martínez and Robert Jeffers, owners of WBJX-1460 AM, *La Campeona*, the first 24-hour Spanish-language radio station in southeastern Wisconsin.

Latino Community News • 731 W. Washington St • Milwaukee WI 53204 • (414) 444-4714

LATINO
Community News
NOTICIAS DE LA COMUNIDAD

Special School Edition of 1995

CANTOS DE LAS AMERICAS
Students Perform Music, Song & Dance

FREE   November 28, 1995 • Vol. 5, No. 22 (#88)   GRATIS

Education: A Family Affair

By: Luis Guajardo

On May 19, 1995, families and educators were honored at Education: A Family Affair. The event is sponsored by: The University of Wisconsin-Milwaukee, Council for the Spanish Speaking,Inc., Institute on Race and Ethnicity, The Performing Arts Center, The Milwaukee Foundation, Bilingual Social School Workers, Milwaukee Public Schools and M. P. S. Participating Principals. Also giving support in the event were the following; M&I Banks, Wisconsin Gas, Wisconsin Electric, and Ameritech.

The program was started in June of 1988 by a group of community leaders, school principals, UW-Milwaukee and The Council for Spanish Speaking Inc.

(From left to right) Mrs. Emily Fernandez with her daughter Rebecca, her husband Mr.

By: LCNN

On a glorious Spring evening a capacity crowd of nearly 3,000 Milwaukeans gathered in the Performing Arts Center Uihlein Hall to celebrate the songs, traditions and dances of the continent's splendid repertoire. Each year

For approximately five years, the biweekly free newspaper *Latino Community News* covered important citywide issues. The final issue, dedicated to education, featured many local bilingual educators, advocates, parents, and students. Al Stergar, who shot many of the photographs included in this book, served as publisher, coeditor, and photographer. After Stergar's death, the newspaper folded.

Since 2000, Mexico native Patricia Gómez, who spent more than 15 years at Mexican public television station WMSLP in San Luis Potosi, has been producer and host for the MPTV production *¡Adelante!*, a weekly, locally produced series celebrating the rich heritage of Latino people. The popular program, broadcast in Spanish with optional English audio, has featured a wide variety of subjects since its inception in October 1999.

Eight

MILITARY

Military service is an honorable tradition in Milwaukee's Latino community. More than 400,000 Latinos served in the U.S. military during World War II, but the service of Latinos in the nation's military has largely gone unrecognized. While Puerto Ricans were segregated in separate battalions, military service for other immigrants was often seen as a way out of the barrio and a path to citizenship. For many, it was proof that Latinos were loyal to the United States and willing to sacrifice to defend the nation.

In the mid-1960s, John Enríquez organized Milwaukee's American Legion David Valdes Post 529 of the American Legion, the first post named in honor of a Wisconsin Mexican American veteran, Air Force sergeant David Valdes. Valdes was a waist gunner aboard a B-24 Liberator Bomber attached to the 15th Air Force in Italy. After a daylight mission over Romania, the plane crashed in Hungary and Valdes was killed. Latinos from Milwaukee have also served in the Korea War, the Vietnam War, in Afghanistan and Iraq, and virtually every other major military operation.

Even in World War II, Latinas contributed by working in Midwestern defense plants, producing uniforms and armaments. As the military expanded its ranks by accepting women, Latinas joined up serving not just as nurses but also as recruiters and working in the supply lines. More recently, Latinas have served in a wide range of new roles in the U.S. military.

Veterans have been at the forefront of social change in the city. In the 1950s, veterans organized around the David Valdes post. In the 1960s, returning veterans were central to the social movements of the day. Juan Alvarez Cuauhtémoc, for example, helped found the Milwaukee chapter of the national Latino veterans' association, the American GI Forum, in 2001.

Born in Michoacán, Mexico, David Valdes and his family moved to Milwaukee when he was two years old. He was a member of the 1940–1941 Boys Tech High School conference basketball championship team and graduated as class vice president in 1941 before entering the Army Air Force. Valdes, who fought as a waist gunner aboard a B-24 Liberator, perished in July 1944, when the bomber crashed after being hit by enemy fire.

Born in Milwaukee, Marcos "Mark" Haro attended Boys Tech High School with his older brother Jesse. Sergeant First Class Haro, who served as combat photographer for the U.S. Army in Europe during World War II, is pictured toting his trusty Speed Graphic camera while Penny, his legendary pet chihuahua, peers from his camera bag.

Carlos "Charles" Gómez asserts his 1921 Kennedy, Texas, birth with a wink, but his red-blooded American patriotism is unquestionable. He dropped out of high school in World War II to work as a skilled welder at Milwaukee's Froemming Brothers Shipyard before joining the U.S. Navy, where he served as a ship fitter, repairing battle-damaged craft. Gómez served on the NTS *Farragut* (named for the navy's first admiral, son of a Spanish immigrant) and the battleship USS *Mississippi* before his honorable discharge in 1946.

Army Air Force private Gustavo "Gus" Valdovinos (left), age 19, got together with his older brother, 21-year-old Army sergeant Salvador Valdovinos for this studio portrait in 1946. All six of the Valdovinos brothers and one of their sisters served the military in World War II or the Korean conflict. Gustavo later became Milwaukee's first Latino firefighter, serving from 1955 to 1986.

World War II veteran Juan B. Torres, of Utuado, Puerto Rico, arrived in 1947 to attend the Milwaukee School of Engineering and eventually settled in the first Puerto Rican community in Milwaukee on the lower east side along Jefferson and Jackson Streets, near Brady Street. Torres and his wife, Carmen, had six children, including John Torres, the *Milwaukee Journal*'s first Latino writer and founder of Milwaukee television station WDJT, Channel 58.

Rogelio "Roger" Cárdenas (right) grew up on Milwaukee's south side and attended Boys Tech High School. He met Dolly, his future wife, while at a dance at Milwaukee's Eagle's Club in 1948. In 1950, Cárdenas became one of Allen-Bradley's first Latino employees. He married his sweetheart, Dolly, in 1953 while on furlough from the army. Cárdenas served in Korea for 16 months. He was tragically killed in a 1977 car accident.

Puerto Ricans have a long, proud tradition of service in the U.S. military. José Quiñónes, originally from Mayagüez, Puerto Rico, migrated to Milwaukee in 1950. In 1953, Quiñónes served in Korea with the U.S. Army's 25th Division, Tropic Lightning. He returned to Milwaukee in 1955 and is now widely known as an accomplished musician and leader in local Puerto Rican culture.

Filiberto Murguía, who came from Mexico in 1953 using his brother Ramón's American birth certificate, was drafted into the army and served in Korea for 16 months. Murguía later married Carmen Valdes, with whom he had five children. In 1973, Murguía was "drafted" again, this time as executive director of the Council for the Spanish Speaking. Under his leadership, the agency grew into a sophisticated community center.

Oscar Cervera, born in Mexico in 1945, joined the U.S. Army 82nd Airborne Division in 1965. Cervera became executive director of Mexican Fiesta in 1975. He was named "Hispanic Man of the Year" by UMOS in 1992. This 1967 photograph shows Oscar with his brother Raúl, who served with an army tank battalion.

Thousands of Latinos served in the military during the Vietnam War and incurred about one in five casualties. Among the soldiers serving was Juan Alvarez Cuauhtémoc, with the U.S. Army 46th Engineering Battalion, attached to the 9th Infantry Division. In this 1967 photograph, Alvarez crosses the Saigon River in a small boat. Ever proud of his service, Alvarez helped launch the Milwaukee chapter of the American GI Forum in 2001.

94

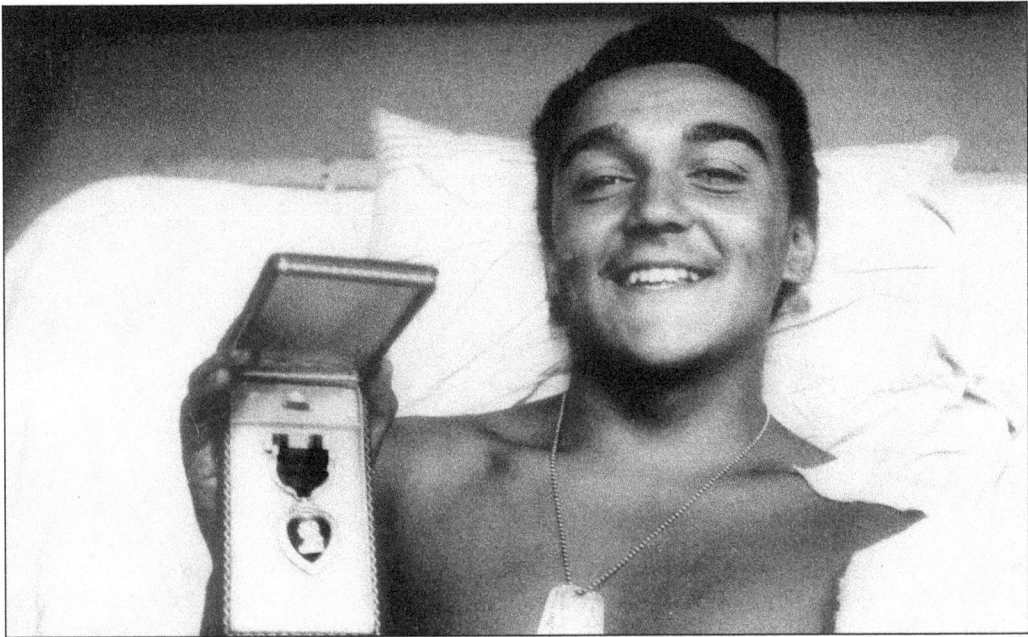

Fernando Rodríguez served in Vietnam as a member of the 1st Marine Division. In May 1969, while defending a Vietnamese village, he was wounded by a Vietcong sniper. Lance Corporal Rodríguez, a patriotic Mexican American, was awarded a Purple Heart for his loyalty and sacrifice May 5, 1969, ironically, el cinco de mayo. Today Rodríguez remains active as a leading Wisconsin advocate for veterans' issues.

Juana Sánchez, youngest daughter of Cipriano and María Gregoria Sánchez, was just 18 years old when photographed in 1970 in her U.S. Air Force uniform. She served at Lackland Air Force Base in San Antonio, Texas, at the time this photograph was taken. Her family was part of the migrant stream prior to settling in Milwaukee.

Angelina Ramos was elected president of the Milwaukee County Chapter of the Catholic War Veterans Auxiliary in 1976. The Catholic War Veterans Auxiliary provides youth programs, encourages people to vote, helps veterans in hospitals, and participates in patriotic celebrations. Ramos (left) is shown in this photograph with floral arrangements at the Annual Memorial Mass held at the Veterans Administration Hospital in Wood, Wisconsin, on May 18, 1975.

Latinos have served the U.S. military with distinction, including Milwaukee's own Miss Puerto Rico 1977, Pvt. Evelyn Montáno, who saw duty as a recruiter aide at the U.S. Army Recruiting Station on West Capitol Drive. While many veterans' memorials exist throughout Wisconsin, none specifically honor the service of Latinos. Milwaukee veterans' organizations and Latino Arts, Incorporated, are hoping to build a Latino veterans' memorial in the heart of Wisconsin's largest Latino neighborhood.

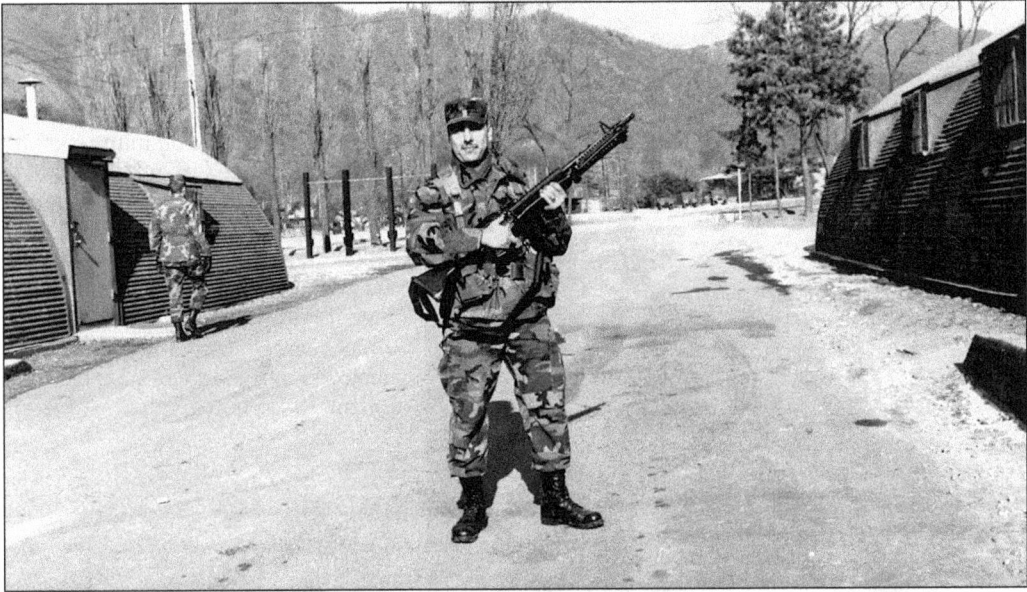

When South Korea hosted the Olympics in 1988, North Korea boycotted. That year, Bernardino Alvarez, from a family of migrant workers with a tradition of military service, served with the U.S. Army's 2nd Infantry Division in Korea. Pictured in the demilitarized zone (DMZ) during a state of heightened alert, Alvarez later attended the University of Wisconsin–Milwaukee on the GI Bill. With Robert Miranda, Alvarez cofounded the University of Wisconsin–Milwaukee Latino Students Union.

While Latinos have long served in the U.S. military, today more serve than ever before. After honorable discharge, many benefit from the training they received in the military and from veteran programs such as home loans and the GI Bill. Among them are University of Wisconsin–Milwaukee graduate student Martin Christiansen, grandson of Félix Martínez Bermúdes, a Mexican immigrant and local foundry worker. An armorer with the U.S. Marines during Operation Desert Storm, Christiansen is pictured aboard the USS *Dubuque* in 1991.

Julio Fontanez, son of María Fontanez Ruiz and Puerto Rico–born Angel Arturo Fontanez, was born in Milwaukee in 1982. He attended Bruce-Guadalupe Community School, graduated from Pulaski High School, and attended the Milwaukee Area Technical College before enlisting in the U.S. Army in 2003. As a specialist with the HHC 32nd Signal Battalion, he served one and a half years in Germany before being deployed to Iraq, where he is pictured in this 2005 photograph.

During World War II, Jesse Haro served in the U.S. Army with the 83rd Reconnaissance Battalion, 3rd Armored Division and saw combat action during the Battle of the Bulge in 1944. Haro has worked for years as commander of the VFW Knutson Post 2304 and the American Legion David Valdes Post 529. ¡Aquí! Milwaukee, a local Latino lifestyle magazine, featured Haro on the cover of the magazine's December 2005 issue, highlighting a story about Latino veterans, "The Invisible Men."

Nine

COMMUNITY ACTIVISM

Latinos suffered for many years from discrimination and prejudice in Milwaukee, excluded from adequate housing and employment. The 1960s saw the rise of protests influenced by the civil rights movement and the Chicano and Puerto Rican movements. Activists confronted city agencies and politicians that ignored issues of police brutality and bias, public schools that ignored or held Latino culture and Spanish language in disdain, and inadequate housing and job discrimination. Stimulated by the Chicano movement and César Chávez and the United Farm Workers, young Latinos—many originally having migrated from Texas—helped organize migrant workers. These activists included Jesús Salas, Ernesto Chacón, and Roberto Hernández.

Several major protests demonstrated the clout of the newly politicized Latino community. In 1968, Latinos joined Milwaukee priest and social activist Fr. James Groppi in marching for more jobs at Allen Bradley. In 1969, the Latino community marched across the Sixth Street viaduct to protest police brutality. Many of the protests and marches were covered in the community newspaper *La Guardia*. In 1970, Latinos sat in at the University of Wisconsin–Milwaukee chancellor's office in protest of university's inattention to the city's Latino community and Latino students.

The activism of the 1960s and 1970s helped bring about social change and more job opportunities in civil service positions. Anglo politicians made it a point to visit the Latino community. Finally, in the 1990s, Latinos began making an impact in the law and politics. Judge Elsa Lamelas was appointed to the Milwaukee Circuit Court in 1993; Pedro Colón was elected to the state legislature from Milwaukee's 8th Assembly District in 1998; Angel Sánchez was elected to the Milwaukee City Council in 2000; Jennifer Morales was elected to the Milwaukee Public School Board in 2001; and Peggy West elected to the Milwaukee County Board in 2004.

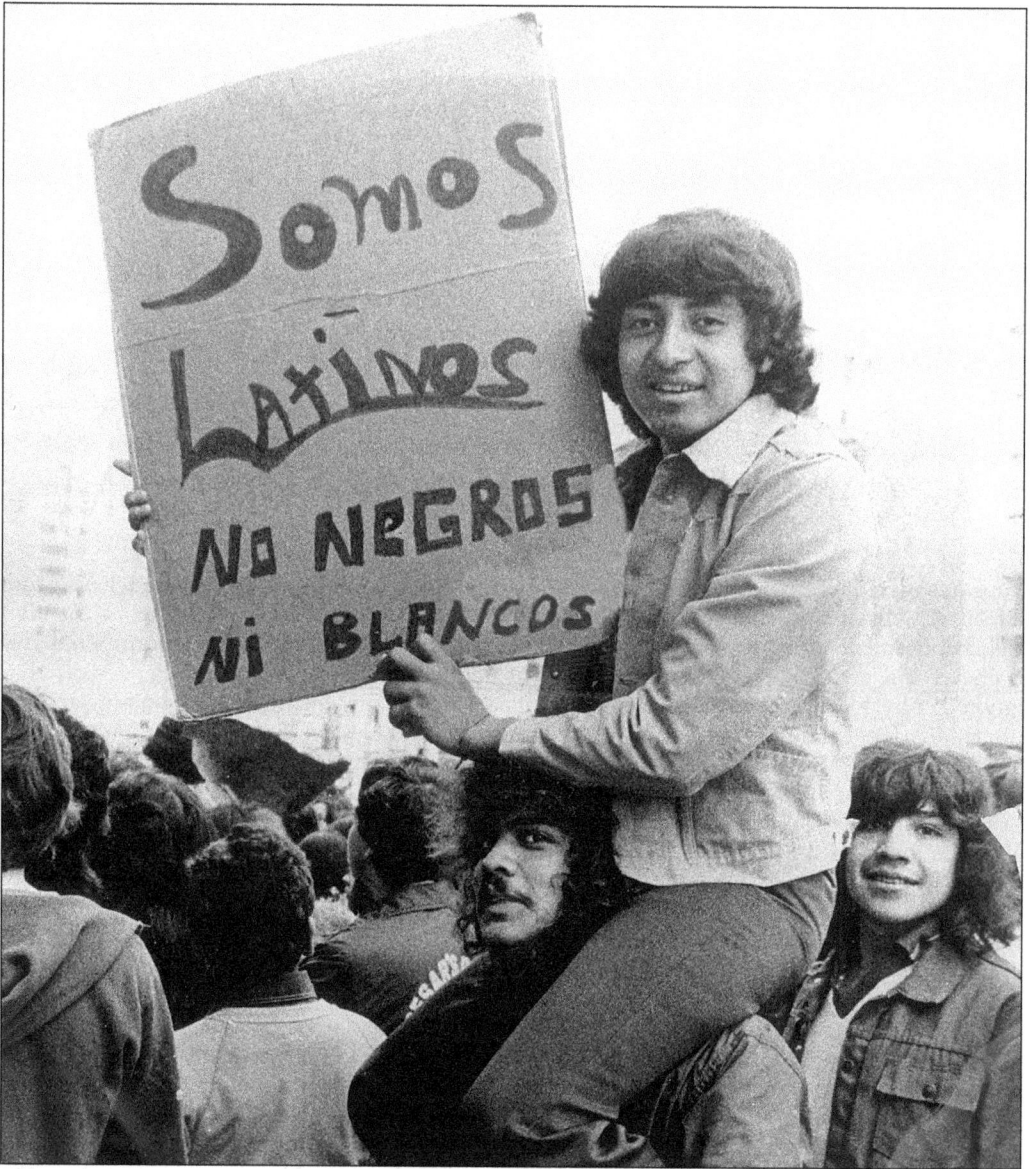

From the earliest years, predominantly European-heritage residents have been unsure about what to call the area's Spanish-speaking immigrants. In 1927, Fr. Joseph Barbian, vicar general of the Archdiocese of Milwaukee, wrote a letter to Frank Gross, the "Mexican ambassador" for the Knights of Columbus, stating that no collections "need be taken up at Our Lady of Guadaloupe [sic] Mission." Barbian added, "I do not know if you are able to include yourself in the collections for the Negro and Indian Missions, since I feel that your race belongs to neither the Indian or Negro race." By 1970, Latinos in southeastern Wisconsin were proudly proclaiming their cultural identity, as evidenced by the poster held by a South Division High School student during the takeover of the University of Wisconsin–Milwaukee chancellor's office, demanding more programs to attract Latinos to the college. Translated, his hand scrawled sign reads, "We are Latinos—neither blacks nor whites." Ten years later, the U.S. government used the word "Hispanic" on the 1980 census forms for the very first time, touching off a still-raging debate over whether "Latino" may be the more appropriate term.

Just five years old and clutching a doll in this 1955 photograph, María Lourdes Castillo later came to Milwaukee with her parents from Guadalajara, Mexico. With the support of her family, who valued the importance of education, she worked her way up through a variety of educational posts and eventually earned the position of principal of Vieau School, now managing the educational and financial operation of one of the larger Milwaukee Public Schools K–8 bilingual schools.

Carlos Sevilla (son of Miguel Sevilla, an early immigrant who returned to Mexico in 1932) arrived in Milwaukee in the 1950s. Community activist and leader, Sevilla became director of El Centro Credit Union and was the first Latino director of the Council for the Spanish Speaking. In this 1971 *La Guardia* photograph, Sevilla talks with Gov. Patrick Lucey about police brutality, the need for education, improved housing, and job opportunities.

In 1960, Barbara Medina, daughter of Genevieve and Avelardo Medina, proudly poses with her favorite pets while living at Horner's Farm in Union Grove, where her mother worked as the first woman supervisor. Fifteen years later, Barbara was crowned Milwaukee's Miss Mexican Independence 1975. Today Barbara Medina is well known in the Milwaukee area for her hard work with several different agencies as an advocate for civil rights and women's issues.

Ernesto Chacón, important in Milwaukee's struggle for civil rights, was active with both the Brown Berets and the Latin American Union for Civil Rights (LAUCR). Chacón went on to serve as president and director of the Federation for Civic Action from 1989 until 2003, when he was appointed deputy director of Gov. James Doyle's Milwaukee office. Pictured at a mid-1970s LAUCR meeting, from left to right, are Charlie Quezada, Mary Ann McNulty, María Rodríguez, and Chacón.

Elsa Lamelas, just 19 years old in this 1970 photograph, later worked as a bilingual teacher at Allen-Field School before following her family tradition and becoming a lawyer. She worked for the Justice Department, the Milwaukee County District Attorney's Office, and the U.S. Attorney's Office before Gov. Tommy Thompson appointed her in 1993 as the first Latina judge to serve the Milwaukee County Circuit Court. Judge Lamelas has been handily reelected to office ever since.

The early 1970s brought much social and political activism to Milwaukee's Latino community. This 1971 march in response to police brutality at a rally was reported in *La Guardia*: "Over 600 persons marched from the Latin American Union for Civil Rights offices to the Civic Plaza in support of Ernesto Chacón and José Puente, and in protest to the police violence in the Latin community."

For decades, Dr. Luís Antonio "Tony" Báez provided a crucial voice as a dedicated, passionate, and outspoken community activist. In this July 1971 photograph, Báez, then minister of information for the Young Lords, leads a demonstration in front of Holy Trinity–Our Lady of Guadalupe Church. Today Báez is an educator and leader for local bilingual education, serving several community organizations. (Courtesy of the Milwaukee Journal-Sentinel.)

Mexican native Salvador Sánchez moved to the United States with his family, going to work after seventh grade as a migrant laborer. He moved to Milwaukee in 1966. In 1971, he served as president of UMOS before opening his own successful business. Today Sánchez continues to play an active role in the Latino community. This 1971 photograph depicts Sánchez (left), Ernesto Chacón (center), and Jesse Téllez during an Obreros Unidos march.

Ted Uribe (center) worked at Allis-Chalmers from 1951 until 1968, when he suffered a work-related injury. The company fired him. In his struggle for justice, Uribe realized that many other Latino workers lacked information regarding their basic legal rights. With Mary Lou Massignani, Uribe founded Esperanza Unida, Inc., in 1971 to represent Latinos in workers' and unemployment compensation hearings and to offer support and quality representation. Uribe served as the organization's executive director until 1978.

Ness Flores, who as a child worked in the fields alongside migrant worker parents, served as executive director of the Wisconsin Governor's Commission on Migrant Labor from 1974 to 1977. In 1983, he became both the first Latino elected judge in Wisconsin and the first Latino chairman of the Public Services Commission. In 1986, Flores became the first Latino appointed as regent of the University of Wisconsin System. He is pictured in 1975 alongside labor leader César Chávez.

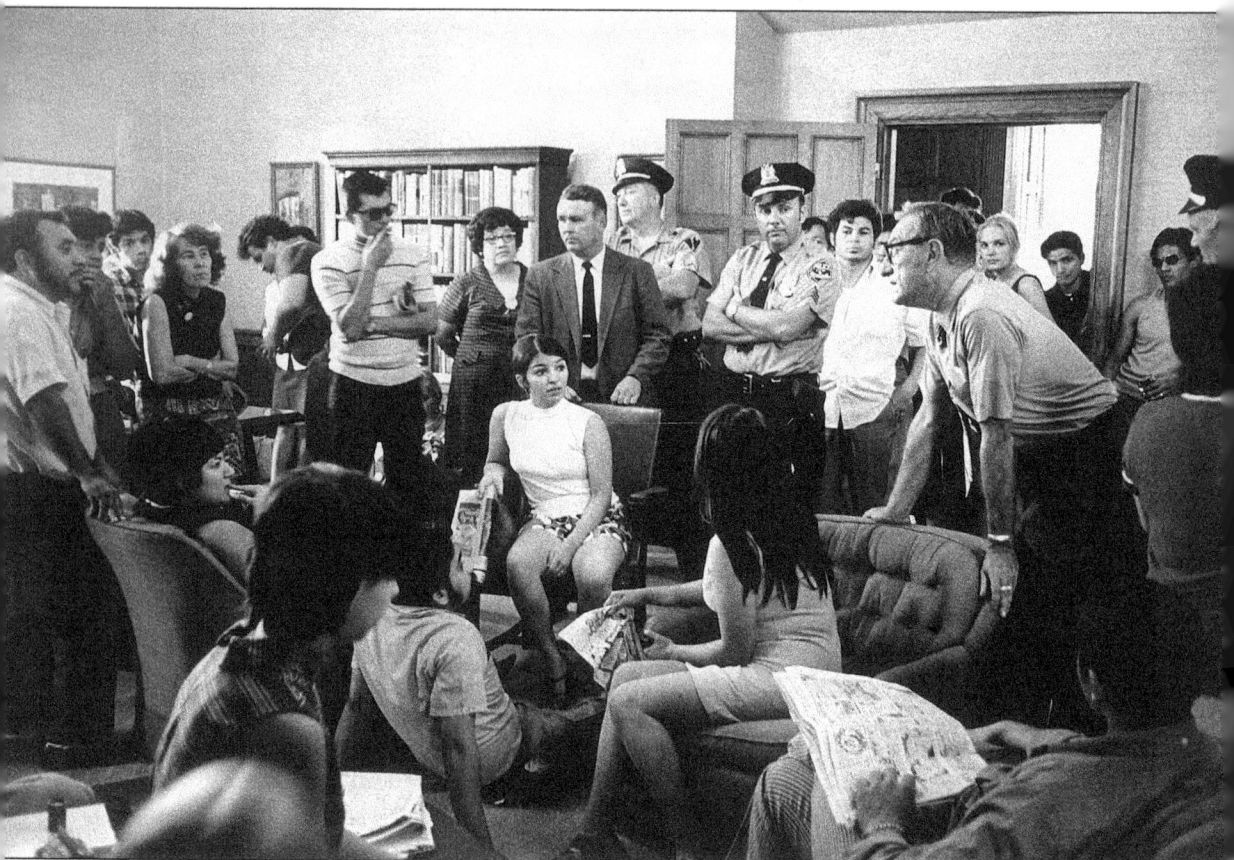

Police harassment of Latino residents was mentioned in nearly every issue of the community newspaper *La Guardia* during the late 1960s. In 1970, the unrest spilled over onto the campus of the University of Wisconsin–Milwaukee, where demonstrators occupied the office of the chancellor. Among those arrested during the three-day takeover of the chancellor's office were Salvador Sánchez, executive director of UMOS; Dante Navarro, prominent radio personality; Ernesto Chacón, executive director of the LAUCR; and farmworkers advocate Jesús Salas. Thirty-six years later, Salas is a member of the University of Wisconsin System Board of Regents.

In 2004, Carlos Santiago, a native of Puerto Rico, became the chancellor of the University of Wisconsin–Milwaukee. He is the first Latino to earn the university's highest rank. Santiago, well known for his expertise in economics, has a keen interest in Latino issues, and he has quickly emerged as a leader in southeastern Wisconsin. A young Carlos and Azara Santiago-Rivera are shown in this 1978 photograph with their first daughter, Lourdes Nelida. Azara Santiago-Rivera is an associate professor of counseling psychology at the University of Wisconsin–Milwaukee.

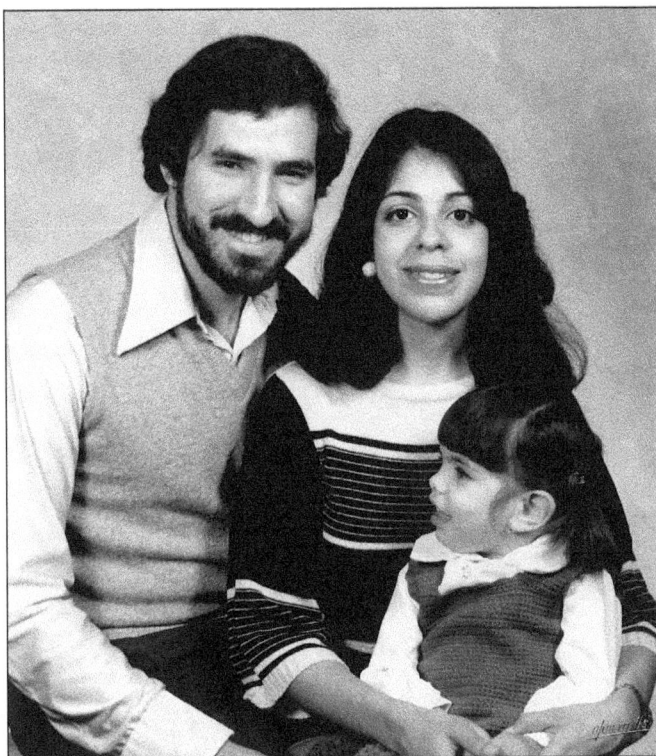

The early 1980s brought several new waves of immigrants. With brutal civil wars and death squad killings raging throughout Central America, thousands sought refuge in *el norte*. Between mid-April and the end of October 1980, more than 125,000 people fled Cuba in the Mariel Boatlift. A sizable number of Marielitos who had processed through Fort McCoy, Wisconsin, settled in the state. In 1980, La Casa de Esperanza welcomed recently arrived Cubans enrolling in English classes.

Community activist Eloísa Gómez was born and raised in Milwaukee. She has worked as legislative aide with the Wisconsin state legislature, as mayoral assistant in the city of Milwaukee, and in several roles in leading area nonprofit agencies and faith-based and neighborhood organizations. Gómez credits her Mexican immigrant grandparents Fidel and Eloísa Gómez for her passion for volunteerism and service to others.

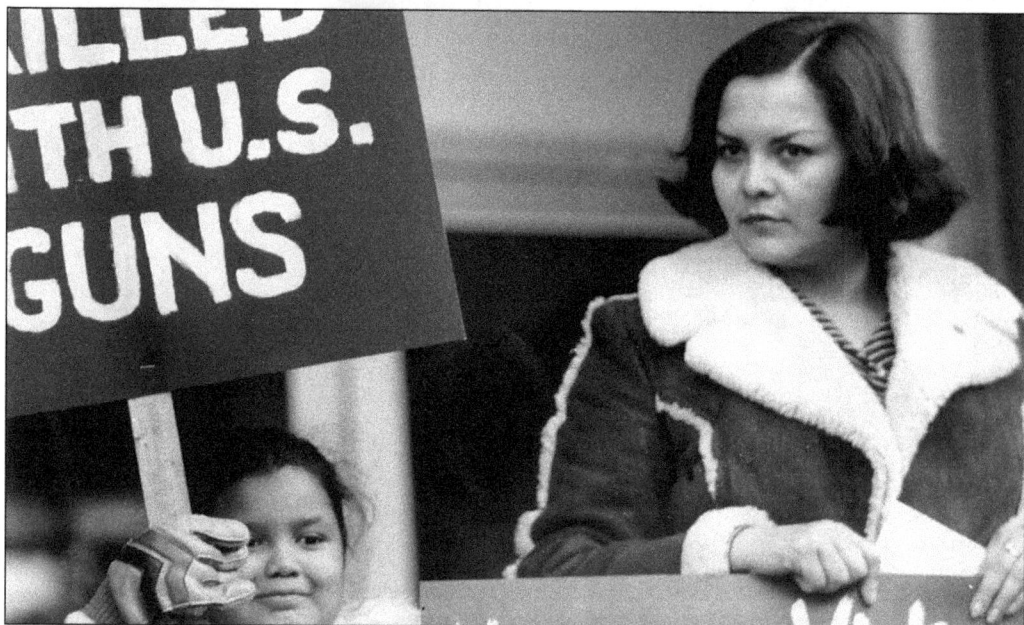

Daisy Cubías left El Salvador in 1965, moving to Milwaukee in 1970. The 1981–1982 murders of close family members by Salvadoran soldiers profoundly influenced both her poetry and political activism. A staff assistant to both former mayor John Norquist and current mayor Tom Barrett, Cubías is pictured in a March 1981 demonstration with her niece Lucy Román, who at publication is community partner with the Safe and Sound program of the Social Development Commission.

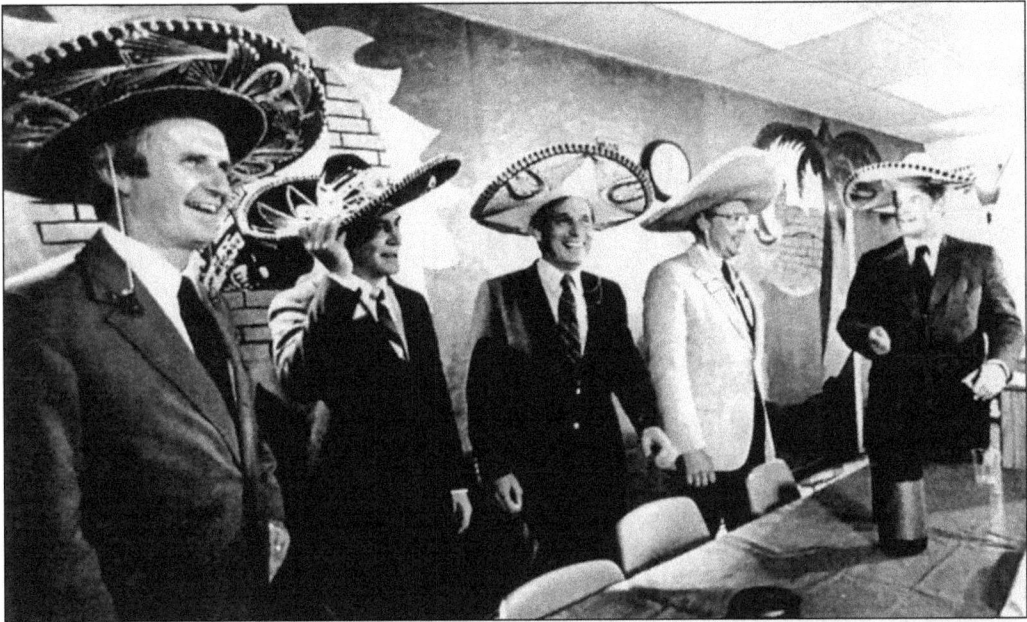

The 1970s marked an era of growing Latino political clout, and candidates thought they understood the power of the Latino vote. On August 24, 1982, about 200 Latinos attended a forum at La Casa de Esperanza in Waukesha, featuring the five candidates running for governor. From left to right are Anthony Earl, James Wood, Martin Schreiber, Lowell Jackson, and Terry Kohler.

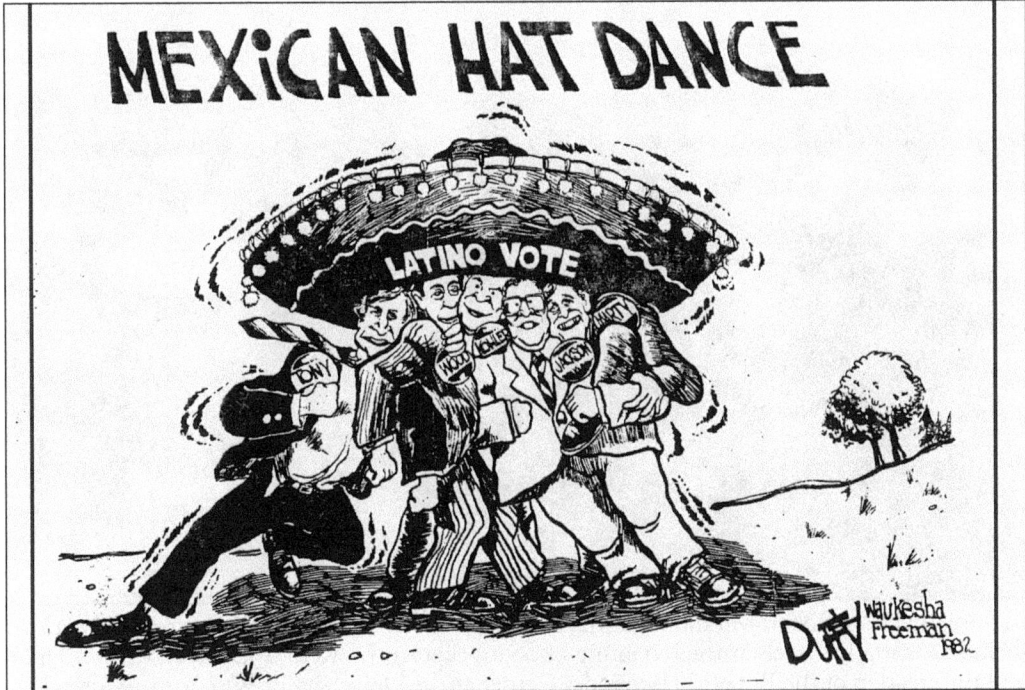

In this 1982 political cartoon, the *Waukesha Freeman* pokes fun at the five gubernatorial candidates who posed for a group photograph wearing sombreros as they vied for the Latino vote.

Aurora Weier, born in Panama, came to Milwaukee in 1969. In 1977, the community organizer led the efforts to create El Centro de Enriquecimiento Comunal, offering free English classes for children, a bilingual alternative school, an employment-training program, and a free children's summer day camp. In 1985, Angel Luís Santiago gunned Weier down in front of the center, later renamed the Aurora Weier Center in her honor. (Courtesy of the Milwaukee Journal-Sentinel.)

In the early 1990s, Robert Miranda and Marshal Vega sparked new Latino activism in Milwaukee, including initiatives such as the renaming of South Sixteenth Street to César E. Chávez Drive and the creation of the Roberto Hernández Center at the University of Wisconsin–Milwaukee. Miranda, an award-winning columnist, is currently editor of the Spanish Journal. Miranda (left) and Vega are pictured in 1994 at a rally denouncing racism. Marshal Vega died in 2000.

Puerto Rico–born, 30-year-old lawyer Pedro Colón made history in 1998 as the first-ever Latino elected to Wisconsin's state legislature. Colón became state representative for the 8th Assembly District, which encompasses much of Milwaukee's near south side. He is pictured playing dominoes with members of the UCC Senior Center.

Rodeo champion Javier Sánchez and his wife, Natividad, left Mexico for Milwaukee in 1968. In 2000, their Milwaukee-born son Angel scored a stunning upset political victory over two-term incumbent, 12th District alderman James Witkowiak. Winning by a slim 22 votes, Sánchez became Milwaukee's first Latino elected to the common council. In a 2004 rematch, Witkowiak defeated Sánchez, pictured on the right in this 2002 photograph alongside Oscar Tovar.

In 1970, Dr. Ricardo Fernández became the first director of Spanish Speaking Outreach Institute (SSOI) at the University of Wisconsin–Milwaukee. Board president of the UCC from 1982 to 1987, he has also served as coordinator of the Governor's Council for Spanish Speaking People, director of Midwest National Origin Desegregation Assistance Center, and assistant vice chancellor at the University of Wisconsin–Milwaukee. Pictured in 1996 with his wife, Patricia, Fernández is currently president of Herbert H. Lehman College in New York City.

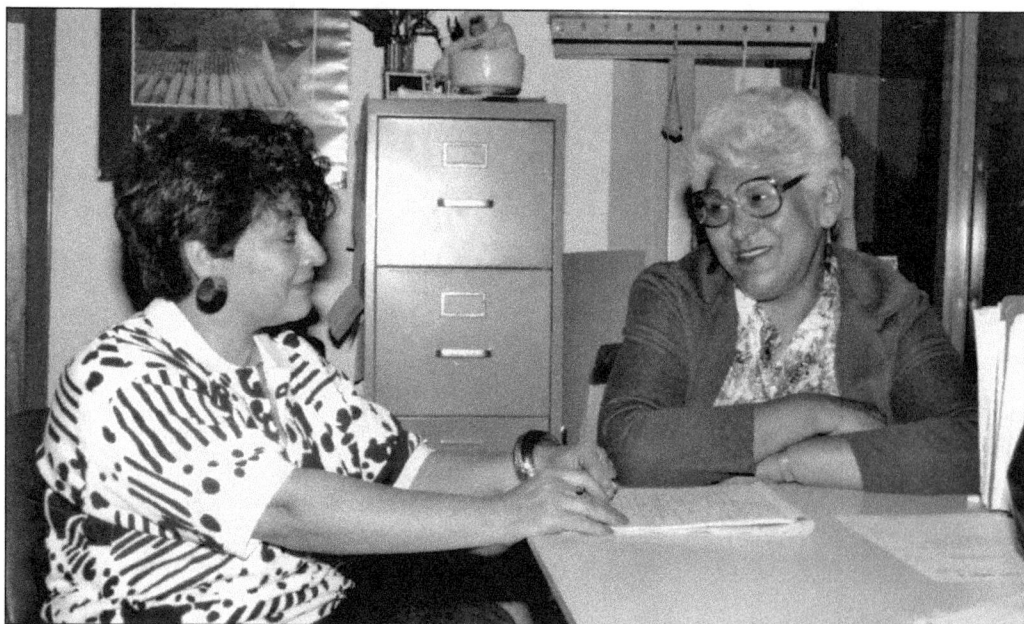

As a married woman with five daughters, Mercedes Rivas volunteered at the Head Start Program at the Guadalupe Center. Although she had dropped out of high school when her father was injured, she later earned her GED, a teaching certificate, and became coordinator of education at the center. Rivas, who was a strong supporter of bilingual education, is pictured on the right in 1986 with Edith Blancas, family services coordinator at the Council for the Spanish Speaking.

112

Ten

COMMUNITY-BASED
ORGANIZATIONS

Mutual aid societies, or *mutualistas*, formed in many Latino immigrant communities in the United States. Mutualistas raised money for the poor, for commercial investment, and for social activities such as patriotic celebrations. In Milwaukee, Sociedad Mutualista Hispano-Azteca formed in the early 1930s and continued into the 1970s.

In the mid-1950s, Mexicans also formed a local chapter of the League of United Latin American Citizens, an organization dedicated to furthering Latino voting. Also in the 1950s, Puerto Ricans formed the Organización Democrática Puertoriqueña, located in the Riverwest area, to help acclimate newcomers to the city.

The Council for the Spanish Speaking was formed in 1964 to provide child care and education services. In 1968, it added a bilingual Head Start program. In 1965, Waukesha-based religious leaders and former migrant workers formed United Migrant Opportunity Services (UMOS) to assist migrant farmworkers. The agency moved its offices to Milwaukee in 1968 and Mexican American activists took over UMOS in 1969. UMOS helped move migrants out of the fields and into factory jobs. UMOS fought for improved work conditions, helped organize workers, fought discrimination, and sponsored community events.

In 1966, the Milwaukee Christian Center opened a recreation club called The Spot in an abandoned tavern on South Sixth Street to serve south side Latino youth. Renamed Centro de la Communidad Unida/United Community Center (UCC) in 1970, the UCC has since grown into the largest Latino-run community-based organization in the state.

Growing unemployment in Milwaukee's south side led to the formation in 1971 of Esperanza Unida, which represented Latinos at workers' compensation hearings. Later the organization developed job-training and other programs. La Causa, formed in 1972, focused on children's issues (childcare, health, and education). Also in 1972, Latino business leaders created the Hispanic Chamber of Commerce of Wisconsin (HCCW). Under the leadership of Maria Monreal-Cameron, the HCCW has grown into a leading Hispanic chamber of commerce in the country and in 2005 hosted the national convention.

Juanita and Ponciano Rentería, who married in 1935, settled in Milwaukee in 1937. A seemingly tireless advocate for social justice, Juanita was assistant director for UMOS for a short time in the early 1960s and helped establish the Council for the Spanish Speaking, where she served as a counselor from 1962 until 1977. Juanita later served as director of La Guadalupana senior citizen center from 1979 before retiring in 1984.

For Mexican Americans in Crystal City, Texas, graduating from high school took extraordinary commitment. Nevertheless, Genevieve Medina did just that in 1946. After migrating to Wisconsin, Medina's drive earned her the role of first woman farm supervisor at Horner's Farms in Union Grove. She later helped establish UMOS, a migrant workers advocacy organization. Medina worked more than 25 years, providing guidance for future leaders in Milwaukee.

The League of United Latin American Citizens (LULAC) wrote to Dante Navarro in 1956, urging him to help organize councils in Wisconsin. Navarro founded Milwaukee Council 380 and served as state organizer, director, and district governor of LULAC. In September 1963, the Wisconsin LULAC councils and a dapper-looking Navarro (center, wearing bow tie) presented the lovely candidates for the Reyna de las Fiestas Patrias at the War Memorial in Milwaukee.

In the early 1960s, politicians began to recognize the importance of Latino voters, essentially ignored in earlier years. In 1963, Wisconsin governor John W. Reynolds met with representatives of LULAC, presenting them with a proclamation honoring the organization. From left to right are Ponciano Rentería and Dante Navarro (Milwaukee Council), José Flores and Beny Navarro (Racine Council), and Manuel Oyervides (Waukesha Council.)

The former Hanover and South Telephone Exchange building located at Third and Washington Streets in the shadows of the Allen-Bradley clock tower accommodated Our Lady of Guadalupe Church from 1946 to 1966. In 1968, it became home to the Guadalupe Center, housing the first bilingual Head Start program established in Wisconsin by the Council for the Spanish Speaking. Today the Christian cross over the main entrance provides evidence of the building's past.

The Milwaukee Christian Center (MCC) established The Spot in an abandoned tavern at 814 South Sixth Street, setting it up with a used pool table, jukebox, portable blackboard, folding chairs, and a small staff of teachers. By the time of this early 1970s photograph, The Spot served as a meeting center, both recreationally and politically, for area Latinos. It later became independent of MCC, evolving into the UCC of today.

Rev. Jaime Dávila came to Milwaukee from Puerto Rico in 1969 to serve as pastor of Evangelical Baptist Church and was soon a leader in making The Spot independent. He served as board president of the UCC from 1970 to 1982 and also as board member of La Guadalupana Senior Center. Dávila is pictured in this c. 1970 photograph with Elvira Borrego, director of the South Side Community Health Clinic, then located at 1231 South Seventh Street.

The Milwaukee business community has long supported the successful work done by area Latino social service agencies. In 1971, Schlitz Brewery president Robert Uihlein (seated) stopped by the Council for the Spanish Speaking with a check for $5,000, gratefully accepted by Guadalupe Center Head Start teacher Olga Valcourt-Schwartz. Also present were the Guadalupe Center's director Filiberto Murguia (left) and Carlos Sevilla (right), then executive director of the Council for the Spanish Speaking.

Michael Stirdivant served as director of the UCC from 1971 to 1980. With his positive, team-oriented approach, he organized staff retreats and developed cohesive goals for the program. Stirdivant helped grow the UCC and its programs and funding despite controversy over his non-Latino background. He is shown (center) while accepting a check in support of the UCC's youth athletic programs in 1973.

Born in Milwaukee of Mexican parents, four-year-old Maricruz Talavera attended the Head Start program at the Guadalupe Center in 1973, at Third and Washington Streets. Established by the Council for the Spanish Speaking (the Spanish Center) in 1968, it was the first bilingual Head Start program in Wisconsin. Talavera later became chief financial officer for the Spanish Center. With her is teacher Genoveva Maldonado, who retired on November 30, 2005.

In 1969, the Milwaukee Commission on Community Relations described its purpose as attempting "by means of education and conciliation, to foster mutual self-respect and understanding among all racial, religious, and ethnic groups in Milwaukee." In the mid-1970s, the organization handled grievances regarding employment, housing, public accommodations, and neighborhood complaints. This 1975 photograph depicts analysts Rosa Givens and Arnoldo Sevilla in front of the organization's office at 1101 West National Avenue.

As a child, Richard Oulahan learned Spanish while living in Mexico City with his father, a noted *Life* magazine correspondent. Oulahan joined the staff of Esperanza Unida in 1973, working in service to Milwaukee's Latino community as an outspoken advocate for workers' rights and job training. In 1978, Oulahan followed Ted Uribe as the organization's executive director, holding the post for 26 years until suffering health problems in 2004.

In the early 1970s, Carroll College in Waukesha began a concentrated effort to recruit students from Puerto Rico. The college's efforts were quite successful, and many Carroll graduates today provide outstanding leadership in the Latino community. Among them are attorney José Olivieri (far left, second row from top), who has served two terms as UCC board president (1987–1992 and currently). His hard work and devotion has helped to make the UCC the success that it is today.

The Milwaukee Christian Center established The Spot in 1966. In 1970, a committee negotiated its independence, and the organization was renamed Centro de la Comunidad Unida/United Community Center (UCC). In 1972, the UCC purchased the parish hall of St. John the Evangelist Church at 1028 South Ninth Street and used the building as a gymnasium and multipurpose room for many years, as pictured in this 1978 photograph.

When Cuban-born Ricardo Díaz (left) came to Carroll College in Waukesha in 1973, Walter Sava was an assistant professor of Spanish. Their paths have crossed ever since. Díaz, who later became part-time executive director of La Casa de Esperanza, involved Sava with Waukesha's Latino community and La Casa's board of directors. Díaz later served as executive director of the UCC from 1984 to 1988. He became commissioner of city development in Milwaukee (the highest-ranking Latino to have ever worked for the City of Milwaukee). When Sava served as executive director of La Casa de Esperanza from 1977 to 1983, Díaz was on the organization's board, and while Sava headed UCC from 1989 to 2003, Díaz served on the UCC board. Upon Sava's retirement from UCC in 2003, Díaz returned to head the organization. Their friendship and unwavering support of each other is an example of the popular slogan promoted by the Hispanic Chamber of Commerce of Wisconsin, "¡Adelante Juntos!"

Dora Acosta, pictured in 1980, is well known for her service to the Latino community. After many years of working at the UCC, she is currently the dean of students at the Bruce-Guadalupe Community School. Her hard work and devotion to her students has impacted the community in countless positive ways.

Oscar Mireles's creative insight boosted Milwaukee's Latino art scene in the 1980s. Mireles is editor of two *I Didn't Know There Were Latinos in Wisconsin* anthologies of Latino writers, and has received numerous awards for his community service and activism. Mireles (right) is pictured with Ted Friedlander (center) receiving a check on behalf of the UCC from Víctor Delgado, R.Ph.

Members of La Guadalupana Senior Center, then at 800 South Fifth Street, demonstrate their national and ethnic pride while riding on a float in the September 1986 Puerto Rican parade. Pictured are seniors from Nicaragua, Poland, Colombia, and of course, Puerto Rico. La Guadalupana was the only area senior center that was bilingual English/Spanish. Thanks to the effort of Rev. Jaime Dávila and César Pabón, it merged with the UCC in 1996.

Centro del Niño, a preschool day care program at Center and Holton Streets, merged with the UCC in 1990 to form the site of a Head Start program. The Reynaldo Hernández mural on the side of the building illustrates the cultural heritage of the adjacent north side neighborhood, home to a significant number of Milwaukee Latinos.

José Ruano (center, holding sign) has been the goodwill ambassador of the Miller Brewing Company in the Latino community for more than 30 years. He is pictured here in July 1992, when the UCC was recognized by the National Council of La Raza as the affiliate of the year. Shown here from left to right are (first row) Sara Morales, Elma Gonzales Radke, Olga Valcourt Schwartz, José Ruano, and Vicente Castellanos; (second row) Lee Martínez, Arnoldo Sevilla, Carlos Sava, and Walter Sava.

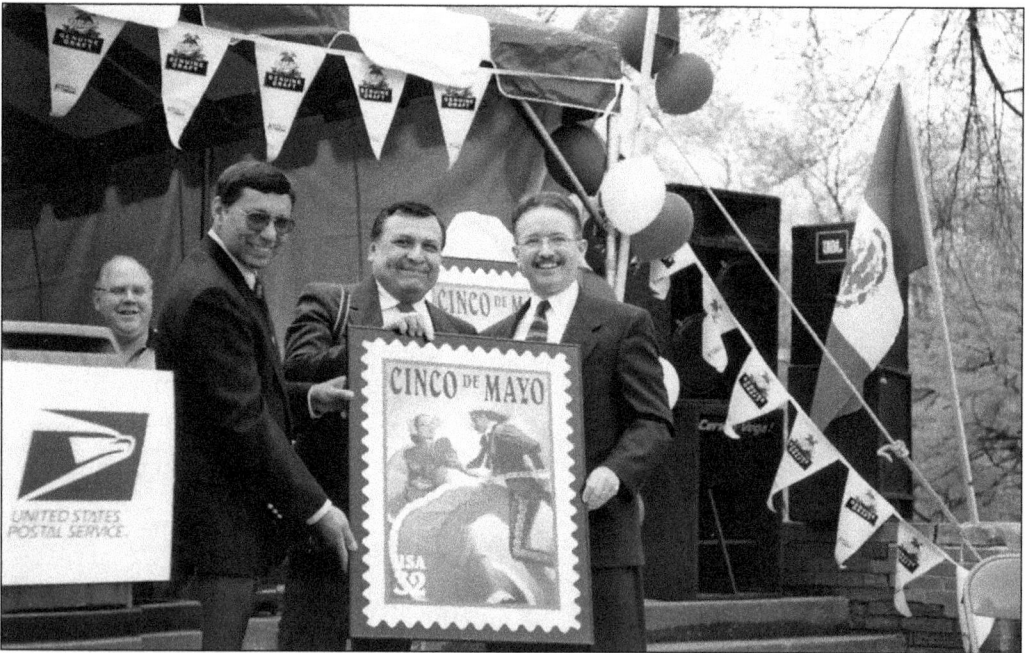

At the UMOS Cinco de Mayo festival in Mitchell Park in 1998, from left to right, UMOS executive director Lupe Martínez, Dr. Pablo Pedraza, and a postal service representative unveil the holiday's commemorative stamp to the nation. Upon Pedraza's death in 2004, the UCC established a scholarship fund named in his honor for Bruce-Guadalupe Community School students.

Agustín "Gus" Ramírez and Michael Cudahy (wearing sombrero) are pictured at the Bruce-Guadalupe Middle School dedication in 2000. Ramírez is chairman and CEO of HUSCO International, Inc. Noted Milwaukee area philanthropist Cudahy is the founder of Marquette Electronics. As two of the UCC's most supportive benefactors, their generosity and involvement have made many of the UCC's ideas and goals possible.

Longtime UCC board members Jack Ladky (left), Ted Friedlander (center), and Joseph Delgadillo (right) have played active roles in the shaping and growth of the UCC and Bruce-Guadalupe Community School, collectively raising millions of dollars. The three are pictured at the 2002 groundbreaking ceremony for the expansion of the Bruce-Guadalupe Community School.

Walter Sava, pictured in 2002, quit school at age 13 in Buenos Aires, Argentina, to work in a shoe factory. He met a Baptist missionary who encouraged him to attend college in the United States. Sava arrived at East Texas Baptist University in 1963 where, upon passing the GED, he was admitted on probation. Sava later earned a Ph.D. from the University of Wisconsin–Madison. Between 1971 and 1989, he worked six years as assistant professor of Spanish at Carroll College, six years as executive director of La Casa de Esperanza in Waukesha, and six years at Wisconsin Electric Power Company. In 1989, he began a 14-year tenure as executive director of the UCC. Under Sava's leadership, the UCC merged with the preschool Centro del Niño, Bruce-Guadalupe Community School, with La Guadalupana Senior Center, and La Casa Evangelica. By the time Sava retired from the agency in 2003, the UCC had developed a broad range of new services to the community, and its campus covered much of six city blocks. As of publication of this book, Sava is executive director of both Latino Arts, Incorporated and the Latino Historical Society of Wisconsin.

Although José Vásquez never realized his childhood dream of becoming a cowboy (around 1954), as an adult he has accomplished remarkable things. Vásquez served as board president of La Casa de Esperanza, the UCC, and of Latino Arts, Incorporated, as well as the director of the Southeast District of the University of Wisconsin–Extension Cooperative Extension, a governor-appointed position. Vásquez's influence and hard work continue to play an important role in the Latino community of Milwaukee.

Pedro Rodríguez, tireless advocate for Chicano issues and longtime host of *La Voz de la Casa* on radio station WCCX, proudly signs his letters "Mi Raza Primero." Rodríguez was the first full-time executive director of La Casa de Esperanza in Waukesha from 1974 to 1977 before taking a similar position with La Raza Unida in Jefferson. He is pictured here with wife Virginia at Latino Arts' Noche de Gala in 2005.

SELECTED READINGS

Akulicz de Santiago, Anne M. "The Puerto Rican Community of Milwaukee: A Study of Geographic Mobility." Master's thesis, University of Wisconsin–Milwaukee, 1976.

Basurto, Elia, Doris P. Slesinger, and Eleanor Cautley. *Hispanics in Wisconsin, 1980*. Madison: University of Wisconsin–Madison, 1985.

Berry-Cabán, Cristóbal S. *Hispanics in Wisconsin: A Bibliography of Resource Materials*. Madison: State Historical Society of Wisconsin, 1981.

———. *A Survey of the Puerto Rican Community on Milwaukee's Northeast Side in 1976*. Milwaukee: Milwaukee Urban Observatory, University of Wisconsin–Milwaukee, 1977.

Gurda, John. *The Latin Community in Milwaukee's Near-South Side*. Milwaukee: Milwaukee Urban Observatory, University of Wisconsin–Milwaukee, 1976.

Pokorny, Gary. "Ministry to Hispanics in the Archdiocese of Milwaukee." In *Milwaukee Catholicism: Essays on Church and Community*, edited by Steven M. Avella. Milwaukee: Knights of Columbus, 1991.

Rodriguez, Joseph A., Sarah Filzen, Marc Rodriguez, Suzanne Hunter, and Dana Nix. *Nuestro Milwaukee: The Making of the United Community Center*. Milwaukee: 2000.

Rodriguez, Marc Simon. "A Movement Made of Young Mexican Americans Seeking Change: Critical Citizenship, Migration, and the Chicano Movement in Texas and Wisconsin, 1960–1975." *Western Historical Quarterly* 34, no. 3 (2003): 275–299.

———. "Obreros Unidos: Migration, Migrant Farm Worker Activism, and the Chicano Movement in Wisconsin and Texas, 1950–1980." PhD diss., Northwestern University, 2000.

Tolan, Tom. *Riverwest: A Community History*. Milwaukee: Past Press, 2003.

Valdez, Avelardo. "The Social and Occupational Integration of Mexican and Puerto Rican Ethnics in an Urban Industrial Society." PhD diss., UCLA, 1979.

Valdez, Dionicio Nodin. *Barrios Norteños: St. Paul and Midwestern Communities in the Twentieth Century*. Austin: University of Texas Press, 2000.

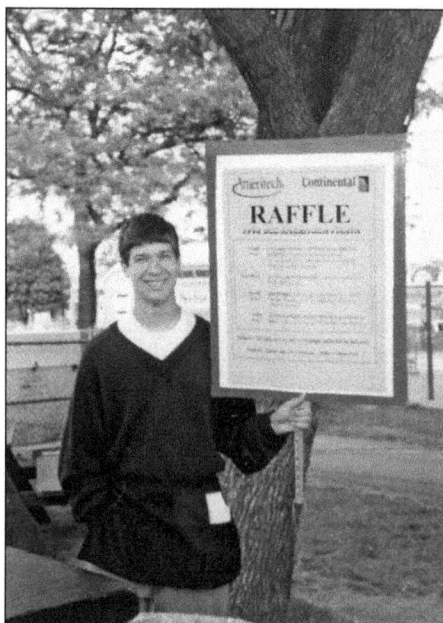

The UCC Fiesta, Milwaukee's second-largest Latino festival, takes place the second weekend of June in Walker Square Park. The festival features Latin American food, live music, crafts, games, and cultural exhibits. With more than 10,000 people attending annually, it has been one of the UCC's largest fund-raisers. In this 1998 photograph, 16-year-old volunteer Carlos Sava, son of former UCC director Walter Sava, sells raffle tickets.

Visit us at
arcadiapublishing.com

www.ingramcontent.com/pod-product-compliance
Lightning Source LLC
Chambersburg PA
CBHW050646110426
42813CB00007B/1933